CONVEYANCING 2005

CONVEYANCING 2005

Kenneth G C Reid WS

Professor of Property Law in the University of Edinburgh

and

George L Gretton WS

Lord President Reid Professor of Law in the University of Edinburgh

with a contribution by Alan Barr of the University of Edinburgh

Avizandum Publishing Ltd
Edinburgh
2006

Published by
Avizandum Publishing Ltd
58 Candlemaker Row
Edinburgh EH1 2QE

First published 2006

© Kenneth G C Reid and George L Gretton, 2006

ISBN 1-904968-12-0
     978-1-904968-12-2

British Library Cataloguing in Publication Data
A catalogue record for this book is available from the British Library.

All rights reserved. No part of this publication may be reproduced,
stored in a retrieval system, or transmitted in any form or by any means,
electronic, mechanical, photocopying, recording or otherwise, without the written
permission of the copyright owner. Applications for the copyright owner's
permission to reproduce any part of this publication should be addressed to
the publisher.

GLASGOW UNIVERSITY
LAW LAW LIBRARY

Typeset by Waverley Typesetters
Printed and bound by Bell & Bain Ltd, Glasgow

CONTENTS

PREFACE

This is the seventh annual update of new developments in the law of conveyancing. As in previous years, it is divided into five parts. There is, first, a brief description of all cases which have been reported or appeared on the Scottish Courts website (www.scotcourts.gov.uk) or have otherwise come to our attention since *Conveyancing 2004*. The next two parts summarise, respectively, statutory developments during 2005 and other material of interest to conveyancers. The fourth part is a detailed commentary on selected issues arising from the first three parts. Finally, in part V, there are two tables. The first, a cumulative table of appeals, is designed to facilitate moving from one annual volume to the next. The second is a table of cases digested in earlier volumes but reported, either for the first time or in an additional series, in 2005. This is for the convenience of future reference.

We do not seek to cover agricultural holdings, crofting, public sector tenancies (except the right-to-buy legislation), compulsory purchase or planning law. Otherwise our coverage is intended to be complete.

We are grateful to Professor Roddy Paisley of the University of Aberdeen for providing us with the pleadings and opinions in some cases from the sheriff court, and for commenting on our text on servitudes. Our colleague Alan Barr wrote the text on stamp duty land tax and offered help and encouragement in many other ways.

Kenneth G C Reid
George L Gretton
24 March 2006

TABLE OF STATUTES

TABLE OF ORDERS, RULES AND REGULATIONS

TABLE OF CASES

PART I
CASES

CASES

The full text of all decisions of the Court of Session and of some decisions of the sheriff court is available on the Scottish Courts website: www.scotcourts. gov.uk.

Since 1 January 2005 all Court of Session opinions are numbered consecutively according to whether they are decisions of the Outer House or Inner House. Thus '[2005] CSOH 4' refers to the fourth Outer House decision of 2005, and '[2005] CSIH 15' refers to the fifteenth Inner House decision. This neutral method of citation is used throughout this volume in addition to citations from the law reports.

MISSIVES

(1) Smith v Jack
2005 GWD 1-14, Sh Ct

In terms of missives for the sale of a house, the buyers were entitled to rescind if the property enquiry certificates disclosed any matter which to a material degree adversely affected the property. In the event they disclosed, among other matters, that a site at the rear of the property was the subject of two separate outline planning applications for the erection of 200 houses. When the buyers rescinded, the sellers sought damages for breach of contract. **Held:** absolvitor. The planning applications affected the property to a material degree and so justified the rescission.

(2) Elmford Ltd v McLagan Investments Ltd
[2005] CSOH 81

The pursuer sold part of its land (plot A) to the defender, retaining ownership of the remainder (plot B). In terms of the missives the defender was bound to construct an internal distributor road and roundabout on plot A. In the event, the road was constructed in such a way that it did not extend as far as plot B. **Held:** that it was clear from the missives, read with the plan attached, that the road must reach plot B, and that accordingly the defender was in breach of contract.

(3) Miller v Maguire
10 August 2005, Glasgow Sheriff Court, A322/04

When the buyer failed to pay, the sellers purported to rescind. The buyer sought implement of the contract, arguing (i) that the sellers having failed to produce a deed plan, he was entitled to delay settlement, and (ii) that even if his non-payment amounted to breach, the sellers had failed to give the requisite written notice of rescission. **Held**, after proof, that the evidence did not support (i), and that a letter from the sellers' solicitors was sufficient written notice of rescission. The sellers were assoilzied. For (ii) see **Commentary** p 59.

(4) Kerr v McCormack
12 January 2005, Glasgow Sheriff Court, A1300/04

When the buyer failed to pay, the sellers rescinded and sought both interest on the price (as provided for in missives) and also damages in respect of other heads of loss. **Held:** that although the interest clause amounted to a provision for liquidated damages, it did not exclude the payment of damages in respect of other types of loss. See **Commentary** p 59.

LAW OF THE TENEMENT

(5) Thomas Dagg & Sons Ltd v Dickensian Property Co Ltd
2005 GWD 6-84, Sh Ct

Some owners in a tenement carried out repairs to common parts against the will of another owner. When they sought to recover a share of the cost, the dissenting owner argued that the repairs were not 'necessary' and so were irrecoverable. It was **held**, following a proof, that the repairs were indeed 'necessary' and decree was granted. See **Commentary** p 118.

SERVITUDES AND PUBLIC RIGHTS OF WAY

(6) Moncrieff v Jamieson
[2005] CSIH 14, 2005 SC 281, 2005 SLT 225, 2005 SCLR 463

A servitude right of way was **held** to include, by implication, a right to park on the burdened property. This affirms the decision of the sheriff reported at 2004 SCLR 135 (and digested as *Conveyancing 2003* Case (20)). See **Commentary** p 93. It is understood that the case is being appealed to the House of Lords.

(7) H J Banks & Co Ltd v Shell Chemicals UK Ltd
[2005] CSOH 123, 2005 GWD 29-557

The defender had a pipeline servitude over land in respect of which the pursuer was the mining tenant. The servitude was granted before the mining lease. Among the conditions which it contained were (i) obligations to indemnify the owner or its tenants in respect of certain losses, and (ii) an arbitration provision in the event of 'any difference which may arise between the Owner and the Company'. 'Company' was defined to mean the defender. 'Owner' was defined to mean the current owner and his successors in title.

In this action the pursuer sought declarator that the defender was 'contractually bound' to refer a dispute between them to arbitration in terms of the arbitration clause. The defender resisted on the basis that only the owner – and not the pursuer, his tenant – was entitled to invoke the arbitration clause. The most that the pursuer could do was to invoke the clause as agent of the owner, and this it had not done. **Held:** action dismissed. Only the owner could found on the arbitration clause.

This case was argued on the basis of contract law, and indeed both signatories to the deed of servitude were still in place as, respectively, owner and servitude holder. In fact the condition in question was also a condition of the servitude. But even viewed in this light, the result would have been the same, for, unless the deed provides otherwise, a servitude condition can be enforced only by the owner of the burdened property and not by a tenant of that owner: see D J Cusine and R R M Paisley, *Servitudes and Rights of Way* (1998) para 13.07. (The question of whether an arbitration clause is capable of binding singular successors is, it may be added, open to debate.)

(8) McEwan's Exrs v Arnot
7 September 2004, Perth Sheriff Court, A516/01

The pursuer owned two adjacent houses and disponed one to the defender. Although the retained house was dependent on the disponed house for access and for services, no servitudes were reserved in the disposition. When the defender disputed the pursuer's right to access and services, the pursuer sought declarator that the appropriate services had been reserved by implication in the disposition. **Held:** proof before answer. See **Commentary** p 89.

[Another aspect of this case is digested at (44).]

(9) Candleberry Ltd v West End Homeowners Association
12 October 2005 and 23 December 2005, Lanark Sheriff Court, A492/05

The pursuer sought declarator that it had a servitude right of access for vehicular and pedestrian access over a path belonging to the defenders, and for interdict against obstruction of the servitude. The hearing concerned interim interdict. At first instance the sheriff refused interim interdict, for three reasons. (i) The right in question being contained in a deed of conditions which was not incorporated into the pertinents clause of the pursuer's break-off disposition, no servitude was ever constituted. See **Commentary** p 84. (ii) In any event a path which previously had been used only by pedestrians could not now be used by vehicles. (iii) The balance of convenience did not favour interim interdict.

On appeal, the sheriff principal thought that, in respect of (i), the pursuer had established a *prima facie* case sufficient for interim interdict, but he accepted the sheriff's view on (iii), ie that the balance of convenience did not favour interim interdict.

(10) Ord v Mashford
2006 SLT (Lands Tr) 15

Land was feued in 1932 subject to an obligation on the granter and his foresaids not to allow building on a nearby field which also belonged to him. The Tribunal doubted whether this was anything more than a personal obligation, but **held** that, even if a servitude, it had been extinguished by confusion when both the benefited and burdened properties had, for a time, come to be owned by the same person.

On the failure to constitute a servitude, see **Commentary** p 88.

[Another aspect of this case is digested at (13).]

(11) PIK Facilities Ltd v Watson's Ayr Park Ltd
[2005] CSOH 132, 2005 SLT 1041

The pursuer was the owner of Prestwick Airport. The defender operated a private car park some distance from the Airport, to which it transported users by shuttle bus. To reach the Airport terminal from the public road it was necessary to make use of the private roadways belonging to the pursuer. This the defender did without permission (though it had attempted, unsuccessfully, to reach agreement with the pursuer). The 'official' car parks on the pursuer's land were losing business to the defender's car park, costing the pursuer around £250,000 a year. In those circumstances the pursuer sought to interdict the defender from trespassing on its roadways. Two defences were mounted: (i) that there was a public right of way over the roadways, and (ii) that to interdict the defender was to breach competition law, and specifically s 18(1) of the Competition Act 1988. Both defences failed and interdict was granted.

In relation to (i), the pursuer averred that the Airport terminal was closed at night, and that during the day it was subject to controls by the pursuer which, in some cases, resulted in people being excluded. It was therefore not a public place in the sense of a place where the public went, and went by right. For the same reason a market had been held not to be a public place in *Ayr Burgh Council v British Transport Commission* 1955 SLT 219. If the terminal was not a public place, there could be no public right of way, because a public right of way must have public places at both ends. In reply the defender averred simply that the terminal *was* a public place but without further averments to explain why. It was **held** that the absence of averments betrayed a lack of candour which was fatal to the defence. The defenders 'have failed to make any averments of fact from which the court could infer that the terminal or concourse is a public place and they have failed to answer the detailed averments of the pursuers from which (if proved) it could be inferred that the concourse is not a public place in the sense required for the law relating to public rights of way' (para 26).

The difficulty remains of knowing what is a public place. In that connection the defender offered the adventurous argument that a place becomes 'public' if it has in fact been used by the public for 20 years. In other words, the 'publicness' of the terminus of a right of way is established by the same means as that of the way itself. Unsurprisingly, this argument was rejected by the court (at para 23).

VARIATION AND DISCHARGE OF TITLE CONDITIONS

Note that selected decisions of the Lands Tribunal (including those below) are available on www.lands-tribunal-scotland.org.uk/records.html.

(12) George Wimpey East Scotland Ltd v Fleming
2006 SLT (Lands Tr) 2

An application to vary a servitude, to the effect of diverting an access road, was granted subject to a possible application for compensation.

The servitude dated from 1988. It gave the owners of various houses access to the A1 by means of a farm road. The road was 500 metres long and 2.28 metres wide. Detailed planning permission had been obtained to build 115 houses on the burdened property. Part of the road passed through the site of the houses and would be awkward, or even dangerous, to leave in place. Planning permission had been obtained on the basis that a 150-metre stretch of the road would be diverted. At 5.5 metres the replacement stretch would be much wider than the original. But it would involve a diversion of some 140 metres, and would now pass beside housing rather than open fields. The Tribunal found that there would be no material increase in journey times and concluded that, overall, 'there would be no material inconvenience' in the proposed new route.

An initial question was whether the case should be decided under the Conveyancing and Feudal Reform (Scotland) Act 1970 or under the provisions of the Title Conditions (Scotland) Act 2003 which replaced it as from 28 November 2004. The application was made before 28 November 2004 but the hearing on the merits did not begin until 30 November 2004. The Tribunal concluded that the new law fell to be applied, but also said that the result would have been the same under the former law.

Under the 2003 Act, an application is granted if it is reasonable to do so having regard to the factors set out in s 100. The Tribunal's 'clear conclusion' was that the application should be granted. Of particular importance were factors (a) (change in circumstances), (b) (the extent of benefit conferred), (c) (the extent to which enjoyment of the burdened property was impeded), and (f) (the purpose of the condition). The purpose of the servitude was simply to provide access. Neither the precise route nor its aesthetic qualities was of importance. The proposed new route, equally, provided access. And it was important, if not actually essential, if the burdened owner was to be able to develop its land. The fact that the burdened property – agricultural land at the time of the grant of the servitude – was now zoned for housing was a further relevant factor.

One argument for the benefited owners was that the legislation fell to be interpreted in accordance with s 3 of the Human Rights Act 1998, which provides that legislation must be read and given effect to in a way which is compatible with the ECHR. In the Tribunal's view, however, s 3 had no application because the relevant provisions of the Title Conditions Act were fully compatible with the ECHR. In *Strathclyde Joint Police Board v Elderslie Estates* 2002 SLT (Lands Tr) 2, the predecessor legislation had been held to be ECHR-compatible. (For a discussion of that decision, see *Conveyancing 2001* pp 35–36.) The Tribunal adopted the reasoning in that decision as applicable in the present case. The relevant provisions 'can be seen to be in the public interest even although they may, and in the present case do, extend to questions arising between two private "persons": the public interest involved is not a direct legal interest of a public department or emanation of the state, but rather dictated by public policy'. And, viewed in this way, the provisions struck a fair balance between the general interests of the community and the protection of individuals' rights.

Some aspects of this decision are explored in more detail in **Commentary** p 102.

(13) Ord v Mashford
2006 SLT (Lands Tr) 15

A field lying on one side of a road was subject to a servitude, created in 1938, which prevented any building. The benefited property was the garden ground of a house opposite, which was held on a separate title from the house itself. The parties accepted, however, that for present purposes the house could be treated as the benefited property. Outline planning permission was obtained for the erection on the field of a single-storey house. The owner of the field applied for the discharge of the servitude (now, by virtue of the Title Conditions (Scotland) Act 2003 s 80, a real burden). The Tribunal allowed a variation of the burden to the extent of allowing the erection of a single-storey house, subject to a possible application for compensation.

Under the 2003 Act, an application is granted if it is reasonable to do so having regard to the factors set out in s 100. As in the previous case, the Tribunal paid particular regard to factors (a) (change in circumstances), (b) (the extent of benefit conferred), and (f) (the purpose of the condition). On the other hand, the Tribunal considered of little importance factors (c) (the extent to which enjoyment of the burdened property was impeded), (e) (age of burden), (g) (grant of planning permission), and (h) (willingness to pay compensation).

The decision contains an important analysis of the new statutory provisions and of the approach which the Tribunal is likely to take in future cases. See **Commentary** p 102.

[Another aspect of this case is digested at (10).]

(14) Church of Scotland General Trustees v McLaren
2006 SLT (Lands Tr) 27

The Crieff West Church was subject to a real burden, created in a feu charter of 1846, that:

> The said piece of ground should be and remain in all time coming the site of a Church or place of worship in connection with the Established Church of Scotland which Church or place of worship should always be maintained and kept in good repair and condition and that no more houses or buildings of any kind should be erected on said piece of ground; as also that it should not be competent to nor in the power of the said Trustees or their successors to permit the said Church to be used employed or occupied otherwise than as a place of worship for a congregation in connection with the Established Church of Scotland.

Normally a burden of this kind would have fallen with the abolition of the feudal system, but a neighbour had bought the superiority and reallotted the burden under s 18 of the Abolition of Feudal Tenure etc (Scotland) Act 2000. The building had ceased to be used as a church as long ago as 1957, but for a number of years (and following a minute of waiver) had been used as a residential lay training centre. The Church of Scotland General Trustees, wishing to sell the site (possibly for flatted housing), sought the discharge of the burden.

Under the Title Conditions (Scotland) Act 2003, an application is granted if it is reasonable to do so having regard to the factors set out in s 100. The discharge was granted. It was said that the purpose of the burden (factor (f)) was to secure a church for the benefit of the neighbourhood. This conferred no particular benefit on the owner of the benefited property (factor (b)). And, now that, with fewer people going to church, the original use could not sensibly be continued (factor (a)), it was reasonable that the burden should be discharged. See **Commentary** p 102.

EXECUTION OF DEEDS

(15) Caterleisure Ltd v Glasgow Prestwick International Airport Ltd
[2005] CSIH 53, 2005 SLT 1083, 2005 SCLR 943

The defender owns and operates Prestwick Airport. On 8 January 2001, following several days of preparation, the pursuer began operating a shop and providing other services at the Airport. But on the same day, following a transfer of shareholdings in the defender, the pursuer was asked by the defender to cease its activities. The pursuer did so, but, alleging the existence of a contract, sued for damages. The defender denied any contract. The basis of the alleged contract was two documents, adjusted between the parties but as yet unsigned. One was a 'Licence Agreement' for the occupation and use of certain premises, and the other was a 'Management Agreement' for the provision of retail services from a shop to which the Licence Agreement did not apply. The case was about the Licence Agreement.

As the law then stood, a licence of land for more than a year had to be in formal writing: Requirements of Writing (Scotland) Act 1995 s 1(7). Although the licence in the present case was for 12 years, the Lord Ordinary had held that, for the purposes of s 1(7), its duration was for less than a year. This was because, in terms of the agreement, the licence could be terminated by the defender at any time on giving four months' notice. (See 2004 GWD 37-759 (*Conveyancing 2004* Case (21)).) On appeal, it was **held** that, having regard to the rest of the agreement, the break clause could not be regarded as altering the stipulated duration. Accordingly, s 1(7) applied and had not been complied with. However, the court allowed a proof before answer as to whether the absence of formality had been cured by statutory personal bar (ie by s 1(3), (4) of the 1995 Act). On that issue the court found (para 16) some force in the defender's contention 'that mere loss of anticipated benefit under a contract will not necessarily be sufficient' for the purposes of s 1(4)(b) (which requires the position of the party to be adversely affected to a material extent in the event that the contract falls).

If the events had occurred after 28 November 2004 the legal analysis would appear to be different. By s 76(1) and sch 12 para 58 of the Abolition of Feudal Tenure etc (Scotland) Act 2000 the expression 'interest in land' in s 1 of the 1995 Act is replaced by 'real right in land'. But in so far as a licence is not a lease, it is not a real right and, it seems, would therefore fall outside the 1995 Act. It would thus have been valid as to form. But all this is subject to the caveat that the law of 'licences' is largely unexplored. The term 'licence' is sometimes used in the hope of circumventing the law of leases. In England the mere use of the term 'licence' does not necessarily mean that the agreement will not be regarded as a lease (*Street v Mountford* [1985] 1 AC 809) and Scots law is probably the same.

(16) Stratton (Trade Sales) Ltd v MCS (Scotland) Ltd
24 March 2005, Glasgow Sheriff Court, CA324/04

The pursuer claimed it was a tenant under a lease with the defender. There was indeed a draft lease and there were averred to be sufficient actings to set up the lease by statutory personal bar (ie under s 1(3), (4) of the Requirements of Writing (Scotland) Act 1995). But personal bar requires a prior agreement, and in this case the covering letter which accompanied the draft lease had said that it was 'Not Legally Binding: Subject to Conclusion of Formal Missives'. In those circumstances it was **held** that there was no prior agreement on which the actings could proceed. See **Commentary** p 130.

[This case is also digested as (29).]

(17) Nicholas v Interbrew Ltd
[2005] CSOH 158, 2006 GWD 1-27

The pursuer, a sports journalist and former professional footballer, sought reduction of two guarantees in favour of a brewery in which, he averred, his signature had been forged. Following a proof it was **held**, on a balance of probabilities, (i) that the pursuer's signature had indeed been forged, and (ii) that he did not know about this and so could not be personally barred, in a question with the brewery, from denying the authenticity of his signature.

REGISTRATION OF TITLE

(18) MRS Hamilton Ltd v Baxter
30 June 2005, Lanark Sheriff Court, A115/99

In 1984 the defenders bought a former schoolhouse in Auchenheath, Lanarkshire from Strathclyde Regional Council. The Council had no ascertainable title to the house and the disposition was *a non domino*. On 8 January 1985 the Keeper registered the defenders as owners, subject to exclusion of indemnity. The pursuer was the owner of an estate which, it turned out, included the defenders' house. Shortly before the expiry of the period for positive prescription, the pursuer raised an action for reduction of the defenders' disposition: see *MRS Hamilton Ltd v Baxter* 1998 SLT 1075. Decree having been granted, the pursuer's title to the house was registered in the Land Register on 8 November 1994. The defenders, however, remained on the Register until 23 January 2000, when it was finally rectified against them; and they retained possession until 23 September 1999.

In the original action of reduction the pursuer had sought violent profits for the period following the date of citation, but this had been refused in the absence of appropriate averments of bad faith. In the current action the pursuer's claim was confined to ordinary profits, calculated as the amount of rental income which the house could have yielded. The selection of period is of interest. No claim was made for the period prior to the pursuer's own registration as owner on 8 November 1994, presumably on the basis that until that date the defenders were the owners, notwithstanding the exclusion of indemnity, due to the 'positive' nature of land registration (ie the fact that title flows from the Register). The position changed on 8 November 1994. From that point on, until 23 January 2000 (when the defenders' name was removed by rectification), the Land Register showed *both* the pursuer *and* the defenders as owner. But only one could be owner. In such a case ownership lies in the person who is last to register, ie the pursuer. (See *Conveyancing 2003* pp 95–96.) This is an inevitable result of the 'positive' system of registration of title: the registration on 8 November 1994 conferred ownership on the pursuer and therefore, by implication, stripped ownership from the defenders. It followed that ordinary profits were due for the period from 8 November 1994 (when the pursuer became owner) until 23 September 1999 (when the defenders relinquished possession). The pursuer estimated the annual rental value at £4,800 and so sued for £20,000.

Ordinary profits are not due if the possessor is in good faith (ie believes on reasonable grounds that he is owner): see K G C Reid, *The Law of Property in Scotland* (1996) paras 168 and 171. After a proof, the sheriff (H K Small) **held** that the defenders were not in good faith and that accordingly the sum sued for was due.

One other matter may be mentioned. All the evidence as to good and bad faith concerned the question of whether the defenders knew, in 1984–85, that

Strathclyde Regional Council had no title to offer. But it is hard to see why this is of relevance. In 1985 the defenders became owners. That being so, it is difficult to see how they could be liable to the pursuer for ordinary profits. (Cf *Stevenson-Hamilton's Exrs v McStay* 1999 SLT 1175; *Keeper of the Registers of Scotland v MRS Hamilton Ltd* 2000 SC 271.) It was only after registration of the pursuer's title in 1994 that liability for ordinary profits began; and, in the light of the successful action of reduction, it could hardly be disputed that by this time the defenders knew that their title was bad.

RIGHT-TO-BUY LEGISLATION

(19) McLaren v North Ayrshire Council
2005 Hous LR 9, Lands Tribunal

Houses within the curtilage of premises that are primarily non-residential are not secure tenancies and so are not subject to the right-to-buy rules: Housing (Scotland) Act 2001 sch 1 para 9. This case was a factual dispute as to whether this provision applied or not. It was **held** that it did. Accordingly the tenant's application to buy was unsuccessful.

(20) Ogg v Perth and Kinross Council
2005 Hous LR 18, Lands Tribunal

A dispute as to whether the terms of the social landlord's offer to sell were reasonable. The parties were at odds on numerous issues including boundaries, access and title conditions. The tenants were successful on some points but unsuccessful on others.

(21) Darroch v East Renfrewshire Council
2005 Hous LR 26, Lands Tribunal

One ground on which a social landlord can refuse an application to buy is that there are rent arrears. The landlord refused an application on this ground. The tenant applied to the Lands Tribunal on the ground that the landlord's refusal was unreasonable. It was **held** that a landlord has an absolute right to refuse to sell where there are arrears, and the application was accordingly refused.

LEASES

(22) I & H Brown (Kirkton) Ltd v Hutton
[2005] CSIH 66, 2005 SLT 885

Transfer of and succession to leases. See **Commentary** p 98.

(23) Dean v Freeman
[2005] CSOH 3, 2005 GWD 9-137, [2005] CSOH 75

The tenant of commercial premises in Paisley, held under a series of substantially identical leases, went into insolvent liquidation. The landlord sought to recover outstanding sums from the defender, who was cautioner for the tenant's obligations. The key question was when the leases had come to an end, the cautioner arguing for an early date. This question in turn depended, among other things, on the validity of a notice of irritancy which the landlord had served on the tenant's liquidator. Proof before answer ordered.

(24) Ethel Austin Properties Holdings Ltd v D & A Factors (Dundee) Ltd
21 June 2005, Kirkcaldy Sheriff Court, A1466/04

Before irritating for non-payment of rent, a landlord has to serve a final warning: Law Reform (Miscellaneous Provisions) (Scotland) Act 1985 s 4. In this case the landlord did so, and then raised an action of declarator of the irritancy. The defence was that the final warning did not contain the prescribed information. This, it was **held**, was a fatal defect, and the action was dismissed. (The terms of the notice are not quoted in the judgment and it is not quite clear in what respect they were defective.)

(25) South Lanarkshire Council v Taylor
[2005] CSIH 6, 2005 SC 182

The pursuer was the owner of Lanark Racecourse. The defender ran an 'Equi Complex' there. She was the tenant of certain areas, and in addition she had a contractual right to use of certain other areas for grazing, but subject to the owner's right to make use of those areas when needed. The question was whether this reserved right of use meant that the contract could not be classified in law as a 'lease'. The pursuer raised an action in Lanark Sheriff Court, seeking declarator that the contract did not amount to a lease, that the contract had come to an end, and for removing. Decree was granted. The defender appealed. The Inner House allowed the appeal and remitted back to the sheriff court for a proof before answer, commenting:

> The authorities ... indicate that a limited reservation in favour of the landowner or a limitation in the nature of the use to which the occupier can use the land would not necessarily be inconsistent with the existence between them of the relationship of landlord and tenant. Plainly ... it would be a matter of degree, according to the circumstances of the individual case.

(26) Warren James Jewellers Ltd v Overgate GP Ltd
[2005] CSOH 142

An exclusivity clause in a retail lease was obscurely drafted. See **Commentary** p 96.

(27) East Renfrewshire Council v J H Lygate and Partners
[2005] CSIH 27

This was a rent review in which the Inner House considered a stated case from an arbiter. The user clause in the lease was limited to office use, but allowed other uses if the landlord agreed, 'such consent not to be unreasonably withheld'. The premises would have a higher value for retail use. The arbiter took the view that the landlord could not reasonably have withheld consent to such a use, and accordingly assessed the rent to reflect the higher value. The tenants argued that that was the wrong approach. The arbiter's approach was upheld by the court.

(28) Bell v Inkersall Investments Ltd
[2005] CSOH 50

Bell occupied property owned by Woodcock, some parts of the land being in Woodcock's name and others being in the name of two companies he controlled, Inkersall Investments and Prosper Properties. The parties fell out. Woodcock and his companies raised sheriff court actions to remove Bell. Bell defended those actions and at the same time raised a Court of Session action against Woodcock and his companies seeking interdict *ad interim* against interference with his possession, averring that the defenders were seeking to oust him without due process of law. **Held:** interim interdict refused, in part on the balance of convenience but for other reasons as well. The pursuer had sought interim interdict

> against the defenders or anyone on their behalf from disturbing or interfering with the pursuer's peaceful possession of the lands known as and forming the Rigg Estate, and that in particular by breaking open locks and chains on the buildings or field enclosures there occupied by the pursuer, by removing the pursuer's stock, equipment or other belongings therefrom, or by placing locks or chains on said buildings or field enclosures against the pursuer.

The court took the view that the expression 'the lands known as and forming the Rigg Estate' was insufficiently specific. The term 'peaceful possession' was also too unspecific.

(29) Stratton (Trade Sales) Ltd v MCS (Scotland) Ltd
24 March 2005, Glasgow Sheriff Court, CA324/04

Application of statutory personal bar to leases. For fuller details see (16).

(30) Thomson v Edinburgh City Council
[2005] CSOH 77

The defender, who was the pursuer's landlord, served notice to quit. The pursuer responded by suing for interdict and interim interdict against the defender from 'instituting diligence on the basis of the purported notice to quit'. At the hearing on interim interdict, the defender's counsel objected, in the first place, that this conclusion was meaningless, and, in the second place, that if the pursuer considered the notice to quit to be invalid the proper way to argue it would be as a defence in an action of removing, since the defender could not get the pursuer out of the property except by means of such an action. The Lord Ordinary (Bracadale) 'was not prepared to accept the proposition … that the pursuer has completely failed to demonstrate a prima facie case'. Nevertheless he refused interim interdict on the basis of the balance of convenience test. The points made by defender's counsel seem unanswerable.

(31) PIK Facilities Ltd v Shell UK Ltd
[2005] CSOH 94

The pursuer was the owner of Prestwick Airport. The defender was lessee of 'a fuel storage tank farm, with associated offices, plant works, fixed plant and fixtures'. It sold aviation fuel to airlines. The lease provided that at the ish the lessee would have to ensure that the equipment was in good condition. The pursuer claimed that the defender was in breach of this obligation, and sued for specific implement, which failing damages. **Held**, following *Sinclair v Caithness Flagstone Co Ltd* (1898) 25 R 703, that specific implement was incompetent.

The action was raised in 1998 and seemingly is still in court. Curiously, back in 2002 all this had already been litigated by the same parties, with the same result, not in a different action, but in the same one: *PIK Facilities Ltd v Shell UK Ltd* 2003 SLT 155, 2002 SCLR 832, digested as *Conveyancing 2002* Case (30). The only difference between the two debates is that in the second there had been some amendments to the pleadings. The previous decision was not cited by the court. On this basis the action could carry on for ever: see *Conveyancing 2008*.

(32) City Wall Properties (Scotland) Ltd v Pearl Assurance plc (No 2)
[2005] CSOH 137, 2005 GWD 35-666

A rent review clause was drafted in a deeply obscure manner, and the parties litigated as to how it should be interpreted. See **Commentary** p 97. An earlier stage of this case was reported at 2004 SC 214 (and digested as *Conveyancing 2003* Case (33)).

[Another aspect of this case is digested at (43).]

(33) Govan Housing Association v Kane
2004 Hous LR 125, Sh Ct

The Sheriff Court Ordinary Cause Rules (OCR) are not the most obvious place to look for the rules about notices to quit (or warnings to remove as they were called before English terminology took over). Yet so it is. OCR 34.8(1) sets out the means of service. In the present case employees of the landlord put the notice through the letterbox. It was **held** that this was incompetent. The proper interpretation of OCR 34.8(1) is that a notice to quit must be served either (a) by a sheriff officer, or (b) by the landlord, or landlord's solicitor, using recorded delivery. Whilst a sheriff officer could effect service by delivery at the premises, this is not competent to anyone else.

(34) Marley Waterproofing Ltd v J H Lightbody & Son Ltd
9 December 2005, Glasgow Sheriff Court, A507/04

A lessee raised an action against the former sublessee for payment of rent and other charges. The defence was that the pursuer was itself in breach of contract, in that the sublease had required the consent of the owner (Scottish Metropolitan) and that consent had not been obtained. (To be precise, the consent had been obtained for the initial period of the sublease, but not for its extension.) **Held**, following *Sprot v Morrison* (1853) 15 D 376, that this defence was irrelevant.

(35) Superdrug Stores plc v National Rail Infrastructure Ltd
26 July 2005, Glasgow Sheriff Court, SE368/04

The Tenancy of Shops (Scotland) Act 1949 s 1 provides that:

> If the landlord of any premises consisting of a shop and occupied by a tenant gives or has given to the tenant notice of termination of tenancy … and the tenant is unable to obtain a renewal of his tenancy on terms that are satisfactory to him, he may, at any time before the notice takes effect and not later than the expiry of twenty-one days after the service of the notice … apply to the sheriff for a renewal of his tenancy.

This case turned on the question of whether the application had met the 21-day deadline. It was **held** that it had not. In itself the case is of limited significance, though it does contain a valuable review of the law relating to the interpretation of time limits. It also serves as a reminder of the existence of the 1949 Act, a piece of legislation that is often overlooked.

STANDARD SECURITIES

(36) Bank of Scotland v Forman
25 July 2005, Peterhead Sheriff Court, A59/99

The defender granted a standard security for the borrowings of a company that she was concerned in. The bank sought to enforce the security on the basis that she was in default. The defence was that the debt was not hers. See **Commentary** p 116.

(37) AIB Group (UK) plc v Guarino
27 October 2005, Glasgow Sheriff Court, A7444/04

The defender granted a guarantee to the pursuer and also a standard security. The pursuer called up the standard security, and raised an action of declarator that it could proceed to sale. The defender pled that at the time of the calling-up notice no sums were due and resting owing. Decree granted in favour of the pursuer. See **Commentary** p 114.

(38) Bradford & Bingley plc v Semple
2005 Hous LR 6, Sh Ct

A heritable creditor obtained decree in absence authorising sale. About a month later the owner sought to be reponed against the decree, arguing that he had a defence under the Mortgage Rights (Scotland) Act 2001. The defender's difficulty was that the 2001 Act works not by a defence but by an application. **Held** that reponing was nevertheless competent.

(39) Royal Bank of Scotland plc v Kinnear
2005 Hous LR 2, Sh Ct

This case was digested as *Conveyancing 2001* Case (56). At that time only the brief GWD report (2001 GWD 3-124) was available. In 2005 the case was fully reported, and as a result both the facts and the reasons for the decision are clearer. After arrears of £10,000 developed, the heritable creditor made an application under s 24 of the Conveyancing and Feudal Reform (Scotland) Act 1970. While the application was pending the defender paid off the loan in full. The sheriff then granted absolvitor. The question of expenses arose. The sheriff awarded expenses against the pursuer. The pursuer appealed. 'Why the pursuers should have thought it necessary to have the "comfort of decree" on account merely of the fact that the mortgage arrears had reached a figure of £10,000 ... is not clear to me' said the sheriff principal, refusing the appeal. We have reservations as to the soundness of this approach. We do not find it 'unclear' why a creditor, faced with substantial arrears, would wish to take enforcement proceedings.

SOLICITORS

(40) Burnett v Menzies Dougal
[2005] CSIH 67, 2005 SLT 929

A couple bought a house. According to the pursuer (Verona), her partner (Alistair) was to repay the house purchase loan. She claimed that the defenders were in breach of their obligations in having failed to draw up a contract to reflect this. As a result, she had had no choice – she claimed – but to agree with Alistair, later on, that she would assume sole liability for the loan. She then sued the defenders for the amount of the loan. Her action was dismissed in the Outer House: 2005 SCLR 133 (Notes), *Conveyancing 2004* Case (41). The pursuer reclaimed, successfully. The Inner House directed that there should be a proof before answer. Last year we wrote:

It is ... not easy to perceive the basis of the claim. Either Verona and Alistair had agreed that Alistair would be solely liable for the loan or they had not. If they had not, then Verona's whole case fell to the ground. But if they had, why did she not insist that that agreement be honoured by him, instead of settling with him on entirely different terms? If she could prove such an agreement in a question with the law agents (which is precisely what she was seeking to do) then she could equally have proved it in a question with Alistair.

The Inner House considered, however, that whilst that general line of argument might be sound, a hearing on the facts was necessary. We remain of the view that the Outer House decision was correct.

(41) Council of the Law Society of Scotland v Shepherd
[2005] CSIH 77

The Scottish Solicitors' Discipline Tribunal made certain findings, and against some of those findings the Law Society petitioned, arguing that the conduct in question amounted to professional misconduct. The conduct complained of was the following (taken from paras 3 and 4 of the court's judgment):

(1) 'When submitting his report on title to the bank in connection with the obtaining of a loan of £61,750, he informed the bank that the purchase price was £65,000, when the purchase price shown in the disposition was £60,000. According to the missives that sum was apportioned to the heritage, whereas £5,000 was apportioned to certain moveables.'

(2) In the report on title to the lender, he was asked 'to confirm whether the borrower was related or connected to the seller of the property. The respondent answered this question in the negative. However, he knew of a connection, in respect that the seller was a company which was owned and directed by the brother of the purchaser'.

(3) In the same document solicitors were asked to confirm that 'the purchase monies including the deposit will pass through our firm's clients' account and will be paid to the seller's legal representative'. The respondent failed to disclose that he knew that the purchaser had paid the balance of the purchase price (that is to say, the part not being lent by the bank) directly to the seller.

(4) In the report on title he was asked to confirm that 'there is nothing else within our knowledge of which you as a prudent lender ought to be aware that we have not told you'. He 'failed to state in his report that the local authority had not yet issued a temporary habitation certificate in respect of either of the two properties'.

In refusing the petition, the Court of Session observed that (para 7): 'This was plainly an area within which it was pre-eminently a matter for the tribunal to determine, with the benefit of their practical knowledge and experience, whether the respondent's conduct did or did not amount to professional misconduct.'

JUDICIAL RECTIFICATION

(42) Jones v Wood
[2005] CSIH 31, 2005 SLT 655

A farm was sold in two parts. The deed plans were incorrect and, by mistake, conveyed too much land to one disponee and too little to another. When the short-changed disponee sought rectification of the disposition, this was opposed by a successor of the other disponee, pleading s 9 of the Law Reform (Miscellaneous Provisions) (Scotland) Act 1985. After a proof, the sheriff **held** that the circumstances for a s 9 defence had not been made out: see *Conveyancing 2003* Case (52). On appeal, the same view was taken by an Extra Division of the Court of Session. See **Commentary** p 134.

(43) City Wall Properties (Scotland) Ltd v Pearl Assurance plc
[2005] CSOH 137

This case is both typical and untypical of rectification cases. It is typical in respect that rectification was a second-string argument, to be used only if the defender was unsuccessful in its argument as to how the document (a minute of amendment and variation of a lease) was to be interpreted. In the event, the defender was successful and there was no need for rectification. But it is also untypical because the Lord Ordinary (Clarke) would have been willing to rectify the document solely on the basis of an informal and incomplete agreement between surveyors acting for each party. It is rare for cases of this type to succeed, for where the document which is to be rectified was not itself preceded by a written agreement, the available evidence usually discloses nothing firmer than negotiations: see para 17-03 of G L Gretton and K G C Reid, *Conveyancing* (3rd edn, 2004). But here the Lord Ordinary was satisfied that agreement had been reached by the surveyors, and that the common intention had not been given proper effect either in the minute of amendment or in the missives between solicitors which had preceded the minute.

[Another aspect of the decision is digested at (32).]

(44) McEwan's Exrs v Arnot
11 February 2005, Perth Sheriff Court, A516/01

Proof before answer allowed in an application to rectify a gratuitous disposition by adding servitudes for the benefit of property owned by the granter. See **Commentary** p 133.

[Another aspect of this case is digested at (8).]

PRESCRIPTION

(45) Board of Management of Aberdeen College v Youngson
[2005] CSOH 31, 2005 SC 335, 2005 SLT 371

A disposition in the form of A to A **held** not to be a good foundation writ for the purposes of positive prescription. See **Commentary** pp 63 and 77.

MATRIMONIAL HOMES ACT

(46) East Ayrshire Council v McKnight
2004 Hous LR 114, Sh Ct

A tenant renounced a residential tenancy, in exchange for another. The tenant's husband was asked to consent for the purposes of the Matrimonial Homes (Family Protection) (Scotland) Act 1981. He refused, saying that he and his wife had separated. The landlord raised an action under s 7 of the Act to have his consent dispensed with on the ground that it had been withheld unreasonably. (A s 7 application can be made by a third party.) The application was granted. It was found as a matter of fact that the couple had not separated.

DILIGENCE AND INSOLVENCY

(47) Henderson v 3052775 Nova Scotia Ltd
[2005] CSIH 20

Letham Grange Development Co Ltd was the owner of Letham Grange Country Club and Resort, Arbroath. Its major shareholders were members of the Liu or Liou family: Shiau Cheng Tzu Liou, Jiah Jow Liou, Dong Guang Liu, and King Hsia Chou Liu, and these persons seem also to have been major creditors of the company. In February 2001 the company granted a disposition of the property to 3052775 Nova Scotia Ltd for £248,000. At the time Dong Guang Liu (also known as Liu Tong Guang, as Tong Kuang Liu, as Toh Ko Liu, as Peter Liu and as J Michael Colby) was managing director of both the disponer and of the disponee. The disponer subsequently went into liquidation, and the liquidator raised an action to reduce the disposition as a gratuitous alienation, the true value of the property having been about £2,000,000. The defender pled that in addition to the price it had assumed liability for various debts of the disponer. Evidence for this was, however, inadequate, and summary decree was granted: 2003 GWD 40-1080, *Conveyancing 2003* Case (58). The fact that stamp duty had been paid on the basis of the figure of £248,000 clearly had weight. The Inner House has now adhered to the decision of the Lord Ordinary.

The different versions of the name of Dong Guang Liu are worth noting. In our culture we divide a name into a surname, plus one or more forenames. The surname usually comes last (though there are exceptions, such as examination lists, eg IDLER, Layzee Bownes). In some cultures there is a surname, but it comes first (eg the Chinese dictator Mao Zedong was Mr Mao). In some cultures (eg parts of the Islamic world) there is nothing which precisely quadrates with our concept of surname. Then there is the added problem that there exist different transcription methods. For instance 'Mao Zedong' is the transcription according to the Pinyin system, which nowadays has become the commonest one, while the more familiar-looking 'Mao Tse-tung' is the transcription in the Wade-Giles system, which until recently was the standard one. There are similar transcription problems for the Cyrillic script (Russian names), the Arabic script, the Arabic-based Urdu script (Pakistani names), and so on. Some people who enter into transactions in the UK use a form of name with a standardised spelling and which fits in with our forenames/surname structure. Some do so only after many years, so that at different times they have different names. Chinese often adopt a 'western' forename not as a substitute but as an alternative, which is sometimes used and sometimes not. Conveyancers need to be aware of these issues. In Scottish deeds the presumption is that the last name is the surname, yet one sometimes sees deeds in which a Chinese name has been given in the traditional Chinese system (surname first) without explanation, so that any third party (or the Keeper) looking at the deed will inevitably get the name wrong. It is suggested that with Chinese names, and some other foreign names, there should be added in brackets after the name the words: '(the first/last name here given being the surname)'.

(48) Liquidator of Tay Square Properties Ltd
2005 SLT 468, OH

This is a case about the law of evidence but may have a tangential interest for conveyancers. The liquidator of a company wished to examine certain persons, on oath, under s 236 of the Insolvency Act 1986. This was with a view to obtaining information about possible gratuitous alienations that might have taken place of the company's property. Those persons objected to the examination on the ground that the answers that they might have to give might possibly incriminate them. The objection was repelled.

MISCELLANEOUS

(49) Cahill's Judicial Factor v Cahill
2 March 2005, Glasgow Sheriff Court, A2680/94

Mr Cahill was the owner of a house. He died in 1986. His testament left certain special and pecuniary legacies to various parties and the residue to the defender, one of his four children. Problems arose in the administration of the estate and in the end the executor petitioned for a judicial factory. The factor was appointed in January 1989. To pay the debts and to satisfy the special and pecuniary legacies, the house had to be sold. It seems that the factor was prepared to be flexible, and to convey the house to the defender, instead of selling it, if the defender was prepared to make up the shortfall to the estate. But the defender did not take up the offer. The defender was in occupation. To market the property the factor needed vacant possession. But the defender would not remove. Hence the present action, raised in 1994. Given the story just outlined, one would have thought that there would have been no need for proof, for it is not apparent that there could be any statable defence: as every law student knows, debts come first, then special and pecuniary legacies, and the residuary legatee takes only – the residue. But the defender had an averment that at some stage the factor had agreed that he could remain in the house. At an earlier stage the Inner House had held, perhaps somewhat generously, that the defender's pleadings were sufficient to entitle him to a proof on this issue: see *Cahill's JF v Cahill* 2001 GWD 31-1252, *Conveyancing 2001* Case (84). The proof has now taken place, about eleven years after the action was first raised. Decree was granted in favour of the pursuer.

PART II

STATUTORY DEVELOPMENTS

STATUTORY DEVELOPMENTS

The text of all Acts and statutory instruments, both of Scotland and of the United Kingdom, is available on www.opsi.gov.uk. The text of Bills before the Scottish Parliament is available on www.scottish.parliament.uk.

Fire (Scotland) Act 2005 (asp 5)

This Act is only of tangential importance to conveyancers. It does not repeal or amend the Fire Precautions Act 1971. But ss 53 ff have some important provisions about fire safety in working premises.

Charities and Trustee Investment (Scotland) Act 2005 (asp 10)

Until now, trustees have had no implied power to purchase heritable property, except for the accommodation of a beneficiary, although such power could be, and often is, expressly conferred in trust deeds. Section 93 of the Charities and Trustee Investment (Scotland) Act 2005 amends the Trusts (Scotland) Act 1921 so as to give implied power to purchase heritable property. This is part of a general overhaul of the investment powers of trustees, which involves the repeal and replacement of most of the Trustee Investments Act 1961. (That Act was already replaced, as far as English law was concerned, by the Trustee Act 2000.)

Conveyancers may wish to note some other aspects of the new Act. One is the birth of a new type of juristic person, the Scottish Charitable Incorporated Organisation (SCIO). Another is the Office of the Scottish Charity Regulator (OSCR, which everyone is calling, with a presuming familiarity, 'Oscar'). OSCR already existed as the agency which, in recent years, had been exercising the supervisory functions regulated by the Law Reform (Miscellaneous Provisions) (Scotland) Act 1990, but now it has a statutory basis and an extensive supervisory role.

Licensing (Scotland) Act 2005 (asp 16)

This Act effects a major reform of the law. It repeals six entire Acts, including, most importantly, the Licensing (Scotland) Act 1976, and amends many others.

Finance Act 2005 (c 7)
Finance (No 2) Act 2005 (c 27)

Among other matters these two Acts introduced a number of changes to stamp duty land tax: see **Commentary** p 141.

Housing (Scotland) Act 2006 (asp 1)

This Act was passed by the Scottish Parliament on 24 November 2005 and received the Royal Assent on 5 January 2006. Its primary objective is to improve the condition and quality of private sector housing. Many of its proposals originated with the Housing Improvement Task Force, which reported in 2003: see *Conveyancing 2003* pp 96–102.

Housing Renewal Areas

The existing scheme for Housing Action Areas is replaced by one for Housing Renewal Areas (HRAs). For an area to qualify as a Housing Action Area it was necessary that at least 50% of the houses failed the tolerable standard. Today that would be unusual, as only 1% of housing now fails that standard. HRAs are more flexible. By s 1 a local authority may designate an area as an HRA if it considers that a significant number of houses are sub-standard. A house is 'sub-standard' (s 68) if it:

(a) does not meet the tolerable standard,
(b) is in a state of serious disrepair, or
(c) is in need of repair and, if nothing is done to repair it, it is likely to –
    (i) deteriorate rapidly into a state of serious disrepair, or
    (ii) damage any other premises.

An HRA may also be designated under s 1 if the appearance or state of repair of any houses in the locality is adversely affecting the amenity of that locality. The meaning of 'tolerable standard' is extended to include satisfactory thermal insulation and safe electrical wiring and associated fittings (s 11).

When an area is designated as an HRA, the local authority makes an HRA action plan (s 3). This identifies each sub-standard house and requires the carrying out of work or, as the case may be, closure or demolition. The plan also sets out the general effect of provisions in the 2006 Act and the Housing (Scotland) Act 1987 relating to compensation and assistance.

Repairs in the private rental sector

The private rental sector comprises around 7% of the housing stock. The repairing obligations of private landlords are currently set out in sch 10 paras 3–5 of the Housing (Scotland) Act 1987, and apply to all residential leases of less than seven years. These obligations are now replaced by ss 12–29 of the 2006 Act, which extend to virtually all private sector residential leases (including those for more than seven years). The basic duty on the landlord is to ensure that the house meets the 'repairing standard' throughout the lease (s 14(1)). By s 13(1):

A house meets the repairing standard if –

(a) the house is wind and water tight and in all other respects reasonably fit for human habitation,

(b) the structure and exterior of the house (including drains, gutters and external pipes) are in a reasonable state of repair and in proper working order,

(c) the installations in the house for the supply of water, gas and electricity and for sanitation, space heating and heating water are in a reasonable state of repair and in proper working order,

(d) any fixtures, fittings and appliances provided by the landlord under the tenancy are in a reasonable state of repair and in proper working order,

(e) any furnishings provided by the landlord under the tenancy are capable of being used safely for the purpose for which they were designed, and

(f) the house has satisfactory provision for detecting fires and for giving warning in the event of fire or suspected fire.

This is a higher standard than under the current law. For example, the landlord's obligations now extend to water, gas and electricity. Contracting out is allowed, as under the present law, but only where the lease is for more than three years (s 16(2)) or with the approval of the sheriff (ss 17 and 18).

Where a landlord is in default, a tenant's options under the current law are either to make a retention of rent or to seek redress in the courts. In an important innovation the 2006 Act allows enforcement through the Rent Assessment Panel, now renamed the Private Rental Housing Panel. The Panel hears applications from tenants in circumstances where the landlord has failed to comply with a request to carry out repairs (s 22(1)–(3)). It is understood that no fee will be payable. Unless the application is vexatious or frivolous, the Panel must usually refer it to a private rented housing committee (ie one of the former rent assessment committees) (s 23). If the committee decides that the landlord is in default it issues a 'repairing standard enforcement order' (s 24). The committee must register the order in the Land Register or Register of Sasines (ss 61(1)(a), (2) and 194(6)). Failure to comply with such an order is a criminal offence (s 28), and in addition the committee can make a rent relief order which reduces the amount of rent payable under the lease (s 27).

Ultimately the local authority is empowered to carry out the work and recover the cost (ss 36 and 59(2)). In all cases under the Act where sums can be recovered in this way, the local authority is entitled to make in favour of itself a repayment charge, which is registered in the Land Register or Register of Sasines (s 172). The charge ranks above all other securities and encumbrances (with minor exceptions) (s 173(2)). The amount due under it is recoverable in 30 annual instalments (s 172(3)). The nature of this 'charge' is perhaps not wholly clear. It is stated that 'a registered repayment charge constitutes a charge' (s 173(2)). Perhaps the meaning is 'heritable security' but if so the question arises as to why that term was avoided. How the 'charge' is to be enforced is not stated. Section 173(3) contains the elliptical information that: 'A registered repayment charge is enforceable at the instance of the local authority against any person deriving title to the charged living accommodation.' Since heritable securities are *not* personally enforceable against singular successors, the meaning of the 'registered repayment charge' begins to look like a subject for a PhD.

Tenants are given a new right to carry out adaptations to the house for needs arising from disability (s 52(1), (2)). The consent of the landlord must be sought but cannot be unreasonably withheld (ss 52(3), 53(1), (2)). The landlord may make it a condition of his consent that the tenant reinstate matters at the end of the lease (ss 52(5)(b), 53(3)(b)).

Work notices

A new statutory notice, called a 'work notice', replaces the former repair notice and (for houses below the tolerable standard) improvement order (s 30). As with the repair notice, the work notice is in addition to the defective building notices and dangerous building notices which can be served under ss 28 and 30 of the Building (Scotland) Act 2003. Unlike the repair notice, however, receipt of such a notice does not give an automatic entitlement to a grant towards the cost of the work. As a result, it is likely to be used more frequently. A work notice must be served on the owner and occupier and on any heritable creditor (s 62). There is an appeals procedure (ss 64–67). If the notice is not complied with, the local authority can carry out the work and recover the cost (ss 35 and 59), if necessary by use of a repayment charge (ss 172 and 173).

Maintenance plans

Local authorities are given new powers – likely to be exercised particularly in relation to tenements – to require owners to draw up plans for a programme of maintenance (ss 42–51). See **Commentary** p 122.

Grants and other assistance

The provisions in the Housing (Scotland) Act 1987 about grants and assistance are recast. The emphasis is on flexibility and on developing forms of assistance other than grants. In particular, the rule that a person who is required to carry out repairs by a repair notice is entitled to a grant is replaced by an entitlement, in respect of a work notice, to assistance (s 73(1)). 'Assistance' includes but is wider than the provision of grants. The full definition is (s 71(3)):

(a) the provision of advice, training or other services and facilities,

(b) the provision of information relating to housing,

(c) making available the services of staff of the local authority,

(d) guaranteeing or joining in guaranteeing the payment of the principal of, and interest on, money borrowed by the person (including money borrowed by the issue of loan capital) or of interest on share capital issued by the person,

(e) payments in respect of any expenses incurred in connection with the opening of a maintenance account,

(f) acquiring, holding, managing and disposing of land or premises,

(g) grants,

(h) standard loans,
(i) subsidised loans.

Improvement grants and repair grants are merged into a single 'grant'. The rules are broadly the same as before. In particular, grants (and loans) will still be subject to conditions – most notably that, for a period of 10 years, the house is used as a dwellinghouse and as the owner's main residence – which bind future owners (s 83). If a condition is breached, the grant must be repaid (ss 86 and 87). So that purchasers are alerted, a notice of the grant (or loan) must be registered by the local authority in the Land Register or Register of Sasines (s 84).

Purchaser's information packs

When a house is being marketed, it will be necessary to make available an information pack including a survey (ss 98–119). See **Commentary** p 124.

Licensing of houses in multiple occupation

Mandatory licensing of HMOs (with some exceptions) was introduced in phases from 2000, and since 1 October 2003 has extended to all properties occupied by three or more people (being members of different families). The current rules are contained in secondary legislation made under the Civic Government (Scotland) Act 1982. Part 5 of the Housing (Scotland) Act 2006 (ss 124–166) revises and re-enacts these rules.

Amendments to the Antisocial Behaviour etc (Scotland) Act 2004

Sections 175 and 176 make a number of amendments, mainly of a minor nature, to part 8 (registration of certain landlords) of the Antisocial Behaviour etc (Scotland) Act 2004. (See *Conveyancing 2004* pp 92–95 for a discussion of the original provisions.) Two amendments may be mentioned in particular. First, members of the public are given access to information from the register of landlords (new s 88A of the 2004 Act). So for example it will now be possible to find out who is the landlord of a particular house, who acts in relation to the lease, and what address can be used for correspondence. Secondly, the Scottish Ministers are empowered to issue a code of practice, to be known as the Letting Code, setting out the standards of management required of landlords (new s 92A of the 2004 Act). But before this can be done, Scottish Ministers must assess existing legislation and voluntary arrangements, and also consult various bodies.

Rights of entry

So that the provisions of the Act can be made to work and be monitored, various rights of entry and inspection are conferred on local authorities, private rented housing committees, house owners, landlords and the police (ss 181–184).

Family Law (Scotland) Act 2006 (asp 2)

This measure was passed by the Scottish Parliament on 15 December 2005 and received the Royal Assent on 20 January 2006. Its importance to conveyancers is limited to two matters. In the first place, it makes a number of changes to the rules for occupancy rights arising under the Matrimonial Homes (Family Protection) (Scotland) Act 1981 and the Civil Partnership Act 2004, and to the documentation needed in respect of such rights (ss 5–9). See **Commentary** p 78. In the second place, it provides, in effect, that special destinations are revoked by divorce (s 19). See **Commentary** p 72.

Land Reform (Scotland) Act 2003 (asp 2)

Commencement

Part 1 of the Land Reform (Scotland) Act 2003 (access rights) was commenced on 9 February 2005: see the **Land Reform (Scotland) Act 2003 (Commencement No 3) Order 2005, SSI 2005/17**. Parts 2 (community right to buy) and 3 (crofting community right to buy) of the Act have been in force since 14 June 2004.

Amendment: access rights in woods and forests

By s 1(7) of the Land Reform Act, access rights are exercisable over all land other than land specified in s 6. Among the land specified in that section is land 'in which crops have been sown or are growing' (s 6(1)(i)). As originally enacted, s 7(10) further provided that 'crops' meant 'plants which are cultivated for agricultural, forestry or commercial purposes'. The combined effect of these provisions was that access rights could not be exercised in cultivated forests. That was unintended, because a previous provision in the Bill, removed (for other reasons) at stage 3, had made clear that access rights could be exercised over woods and forests. The mistake is cured by the **Land Reform (Scotland) Act 2003 (Modification) Order 2005, SSI 2005/65**. This deletes the word 'forestry' in s 7(10), while adding to that provision a new para (c) as follows:

> For the purposes of section 6(1)(i) above land on which crops are growing –
> …
> (c) does not include land used wholly or mainly –
>   (i)   as woodland or an orchard, or
>   (ii) for the growing of trees;
> but does include land used wholly for the cultivation of tree seedlings in beds.

The result is to make clear that access rights can, after all, be exercised over woods and forests.

Summary applications: procedure

The **Act of Sederunt (Summary Applications, Statutory Applications and Appeals etc Rules) Amendment (Land Reform (Scotland) Act 2003) 2005, SSI**

2005/61 adds a new part XXVIII to the Act of Sederunt (Summary Applications, Statutory Applications and Appeals etc Rules) 1999, SI 1999/929. This makes provision about (i) appeals by owners against notices under s 14(2) (requiring removal of notices, fences etc), (ii) appeals by owners against notices under s 15(2) (requiring action in respect of fences etc likely to cause injury), and (iii) declarations under s 28(1), (2) (declarations that land is or is not subject to access rights etc). Among other things it provides that owners must advertise the application in a local newspaper.

Building (Scotland) Act 2003 (asp 8)

Commencement

On 1 May 2005 the Building (Scotland) Act 1959 was replaced by the new Act of 2003. See **Building (Scotland) Act 2003 (Commencement No 1, Transitional Provisions and Savings) Order 2004, SSI 2004/404**. The 2003 Act is summarised at pp 85–88 of *Conveyancing 2003*.

Not quite all of the Act is in force. Section 6, substituting building standards assessments for letters of comfort, needs to be supplemented by regulations and has yet to be commenced. On s 6, see Anderson (2005) 73 *Scottish Law Gazette* 12. However, it seems that no new letters of comfort will now be issued: for the current position in different local authorities see the solicitors' section of the Law Society's website (www.lawscot.org.uk) under conveyancing essentials/ unauthorised alterations.

Scottish Building Standards Agency

The new system is overseen by a new body, the Scottish Building Standards Agency (www.sbsa.gov.uk). Building warrants will now be issued by 'verifiers' but, for the present at least, the only verifiers are local authorities. Verifiers also deal with completion certificates, but instead of such certificates being 'issued' by the local authority (as under the previous law), the authority will instead 'accept' a certificate drawn up by the person responsible for the work. This change in formulation is so as to make it clear that it is the responsibility of those carrying out the work to comply with the building regulations.

The Act also provides for 'certifiers' – in practice qualified and experienced building professionals. The use of a certifier is optional but is likely to smooth the way to a completion certificate. The system is explained by the Scottish Building Standards Agency in a note which appeared in the *Journal of the Law Society of Scotland* in April 2005 (p 43):

> Certification is an optional procedure and it may only be undertaken by an approved certifier of design or of construction. The Agency will maintain an online certification register which will be the only authoritative source of information about certification schemes, approved bodies and certifiers. The certificate is a declaration by the certifier that the work complies with building regulations; certified work will not be inspected

by the verifier. The verifier will, however, undertake enquiries to check that the person signing the certificate is registered under an appropriate scheme.

Prescribed forms

Section 36 of the Act says that 'the Scottish Ministers may by regulations make provision as to the form and content of any application, warrant, certificate, notice or document authorised or required to be used under or for the purposes of this Act'. This has now been done by the **Building (Forms) (Scotland) Regulations 2005, SSI 2005/172**. The prescribed forms are for:

Building Warrant
Amendment to Building Warrant
Extension of Period of Validity of Building Warrant
Extension of Period of Use of Limited Life Building
Completion Certificate – Submission
Completion Certificate where No Building Warrant Obtained - Submission
Completion Certificate for Local Authority Use
Building Regulations Compliance Notice
Continuing Requirement Enforcement Notice
Building Warrant Enforcement Notice
Defective Building Notice
Dangerous Building Notice
Notice of Intention to Enter Premises
Authority to Enter Premises
Certificate to Accompany Application for Warrant to Exercise Powers of Entry,
    Inspection or Testing
Notice to Remove from a Building.

Antisocial Behaviour etc (Scotland) Act 2004 (asp 8)

Parts 7 and 8 of this 2004 Act were discussed in *Conveyancing 2004* pp 91–95. Since then amendments have been made by the Housing (Scotland) Act 2006 ss 175 and 176: see p 29 above. Further amendments and amplifications are contained in the statutory instruments noted below.

Part 7: antisocial behaviour notices

Part 7 of the 2004 Act provides powers for local authorities to serve antisocial behaviour notices on landlords requiring them to take steps to manage antisocial behaviour at or around a house let by that landlord. The statutory instruments which follow have been made in relation to this part.

The **Antisocial Behaviour Notice (Appeals against Order as to Rent Payable) (Scotland) Regulations 2005, SSI 2005/560** are designed to ensure that, where a sheriff orders that no rent should be payable, and the landlord appeals, the tenant is aware that the decision has been appealed so that he or she can set aside money that would otherwise have been payable as rent, in case the appeal is successful. If the landlord does not notify the tenant of the matters prescribed in the instrument and in the way prescribed, the Act provides that the sheriff principal, if granting the appeal, cannot order back-rent to be paid from the date on which the rent ceased to be payable.

The **Antisocial Behaviour Notice (Management Control Orders) (Scotland) Regulations 2005, SSI 2005/561** specify what expenditure local authorities may incur while a house is subject to a management control order and how they can recover that expenditure. The instrument permits the local authority to incur necessary and reasonable costs for day-to-day management activities, whether it manages the house itself or through an agent, together with the cost of routine maintenance. The same applies to the cost of works to improve the house or elements of the house to the tolerable standard. The cost of other works should not be incurred without the owner's consent. Costs incurred will be deducted from the rent but if they exceed the income from letting, they should be recovered in the normal way as a debt.

The **Antisocial Behaviour Notice (Landlord Liability) (Scotland) Regulations 2005, SSI 2005/562** specify when and how local authorities can recover costs that they have incurred in dealing with antisocial behaviour following the failure of the landlord to take the action specified in an antisocial behaviour notice. They require the local authority to give notice that it intends to take those steps, with an indication of the cost, to encourage the landlord to take the necessary action. If the local authority decides to proceed it can recover its actual costs including administrative costs and overheads.

The **Antisocial Behaviour Notice (Advice and Assistance) (Scotland) Regulations 2005, SSI 2005/563** require a local authority to provide advice and assistance to a landlord before serving an antisocial behaviour notice. The intention is to avoid unnecessary formal action if the landlord's management of the situation can be improved by suitable advice and assistance as specified in the instrument.

Part 8: registration of residential private landlords

Part 8 of the Act makes provision for the establishment, by local authority area, of registers of residential landlords. It is an offence to let a house without being registered, unless the house is excluded from the requirement, or the landlord's application is being processed. The statutory instruments which follow have been made in relation to this part.

The **Private Landlord Registration (Information and Fees) (Scotland) Regulations 2005, SSI 2005/558** specify further information that applicants for registration should provide, beyond that already required by s 83(1) of the Act. As amended by s 176(3) of the Housing (Scotland) Act 2006, s 83(1) requires an applicant to provide, where relevant, the name and address of the owner and agent, the addresses of properties let, and a contact address. The additional information specified in the instrument includes convictions which are relevant in terms of the considerations set out in s 85 of the Act. The instrument also lays down a standard method for a local authority to set a principal fee and then specifies how to determine, in relation to the principal fee, additional fees and discounts according to the nature and circumstances of the application.

The **Private Landlord Registration (Appeals against Decision as to Rent Payable) (Scotland) Regulations 2005, SSI 2005/559** ensure that, where the local authority serves a notice that no rent should be payable and the landlord appeals, the tenant is aware that the penalty has been appealed and that he or she should set aside money that would otherwise have been payable as rent, in case the appeal is successful. If the landlord does not notify the tenant of the matters prescribed in the instrument and in the way prescribed, the Act provides that the court, if granting the appeal, cannot order back-rent to be paid from the date on which the rent ceased to be payable. Similar provision is made for where a notice that no rent should be payable is in force and the landlord appeals against a refusal by the local authority to revoke the notice.

The **Private Landlord Registration (Advice and Assistance) (Scotland) Regulations 2005, SSI 2005/557** require local authorities to provide advice and assistance (i) to applicants on good practice in letting houses, and (ii) to tenants and occupants when the local authority decides to refuse or remove a landlord's registration or serve a notice that no rent is payable.

The **Private Landlord Registration (Modification) (Scotland) Order 2005, SSI 2005/650** adds to the exemptions from registration contained in s 83(6) of the Act by inserting new paras (e)–(l):

  (e) the house is the only or main residence of the relevant person;

  (f) the house is –

      (i) on agricultural land which is land comprised in a lease constituting a 1991 Act tenancy within the meaning of the Agricultural Holdings (Scotland) Act 2003 or comprised in a lease constituting a short limited duration tenancy or limited duration tenancy (within the meaning of that Act); and

      (ii) occupied by the tenant of the relevant lease;

  (g) the house is on a croft (within the meaning of section 3 of the Crofters (Scotland) Act 1993;

  (h) the house is –

      (i) on a holding to which any of the provisions of the Small Landholders (Scotland) Acts 1886 to 1931 applies;

      (ii) not situated in the crofting counties (within the meaning of the Crofters (Scotland) Act 1993); and

      (iii) occupied by the landholder;

  (i) the house is occupied by virtue of a liferent;

  (j) the house is –

      (i) owned by an organisation which has the advancement of religion as its principal purpose and the regular holding of worship as its principal activity; and

      (ii) occupied by a person whose principal responsibility is the leading of members of the organisation in worship and preaching the faith of that organisation;

(k) the house is part of an estate of a deceased person and has been held by an executor for a period not exceeding 6 months from the date of death; or

(l) the house is in the lawful possession of a heritable creditor and has been held by that creditor for a period not exceeding 6 months from the date of possession.

Of particular note is para (e) which exempts resident landlords. But if there are three or more unrelated lodgers the house is an HMO and requires to be licensed as such, under the Housing (Scotland) Act 2006 part 5: see p 29 above.

Commencement of Civil Partnership Act 2004

Part 3 of the Civil Partnership Act, which contains the main provisions applying to Scotland, was commenced on 5 December 2005: see the **Civil Partnership Act 2004 (Commencement No 2) (Scotland) Order 2005, SSI 2005/604**.

Fees in the Property Registers

Some changes to the level of fees charged by Registers of Scotland are made, with effect from 28 November 2005, by the **Fees in the Registers of Scotland Amendment Order 2005, SSI 2005/580,** amending the Fees in the Registers of Scotland Order 1995, SI 1995/1945. This follows the Fees in the Registers of Scotland Amendment Order 2004, SSI 2004/507, discussed in *Conveyancing 2004* p 38. The new fees only affect the obtaining of information from the Registers. The new fees are:

Register of Sasines

Search in the Presentment Book (per item searched for)	£1.65
Search in the Minute Book (per item searched for)	£1.65
Each search sheet viewed	£1.65

Land Register

Search of the Application Record (per item searched for)	£3.30
Search of the title sheet (per item searched for)	£3.30
Per view of a title sheet for an interest in land	£3.30
Per Index Map search	£1.65
Per property price search	£3.30

Chancery and Judicial Registers

Search in the Register of Deeds or Register of Judgments	£1.65
Search against up to 6 names in the Register of Inhibitions	£1.65

Land Register Reports

Forms 10, 12, 14, P16 and P17	£27.00
Forms 11 and 13	£15.00
Form 10/P16 and Form 12/P17	£40.00

Miscellaneous services

Provision of a plan or duplicate copy deed	£16.50
Provision of a certified copy or official extract of deed	£20.70
Provision of office copy	£25.00
Provision of Sasine deed	£9.00
For additional copies	£ 6.00
Provision of Land Register archive information per deed	£14.20
Provision of a copy of minutes of Register of Inhibitions (per day)	£21.00

Right to buy

The **Right to Purchase (Prescribed Persons) (Scotland) Amendment Order 2005, SSI 2005/275** makes minor changes to the Right to Purchase (Prescribed Persons) (Scotland) Order 1993, SI 1993/1625.

Scottish Homes

The **Housing (Scotland) Act 2001 (Transfer of Scottish Homes Property and Liabilities) Order 2005, SSI 2005/439** and the **Scottish Homes (Dissolution) Order 2005, SSI 2005/609** dissolve Scottish Homes, transferring any remaining assets and liabilities to the Scottish Ministers. This completes the process begun by the Housing (Scotland) Act 2001 s 84. Scottish Homes, previously known as the Scottish Special Housing Association (SSHA), was founded in 1937, so this is the end of an old song.

Contaminated land

The **Contaminated Land (Scotland) Regulations 2005, SSI 2005/658** amend not only the Contaminated Land (Scotland) Regulations 2000, SSI 2000/178, but also the Environmental Protection Act 1990 itself.

PART III
OTHER MATERIAL

OTHER MATERIAL

Bankruptcy and Diligence etc (Scotland) Bill

The Bankruptcy and Diligence etc (Scotland) Bill was introduced on 21 November 2005. If enacted, it will be of importance to conveyancers in a number of respects.

Discharge from sequestration

The standard period for discharge is reduced from three years to one. (This would adopt the recent change made in England.)

Heritable property

There are new provisions whereby heritable property will be taken out of the sequestration if, after a certain period, the trustee has done nothing about it.

Standard securities by companies

Under current law, a standard security granted by a company must be registered not only in the Land Register (or Sasine Register) but also in the Companies Register. The Bill abolishes the requirement of registration in the Companies Register. The change needs parallel Westminster legislation. It is believed that the Government is to introduce the necessary amendments into the Company Law Reform Bill, currently in the UK Parliament.

Court officers

Though not specifically a conveyancing matter, conveyancers have sufficient contact with officers of court to wish to know that sheriff officers and messengers at arms are to be merged into a single profession, and will be known as messengers of court.

Inhibition

Numerous changes are made to the law of inhibition. One provision of interest to conveyancers which is to be enacted on a 'for the avoidance of doubt' basis (for it is probably existing law anyway) is that a right to reduce a breach of inhibition prescribes 20 years after the breach. Thus if Tom inhibits Dick in 2007, and Dick dispones to Harry in 2009, Tom has the right to reduce that disposition until 2029, even though the inhibition itself prescribed in 2012. This point is perhaps not sufficiently widely understood by conveyancers.

A terminological change is that the Register of Inhibitions and Adjudications is renamed the Register of Inhibitions.

Abolition of adjudication

Adjudication for debt is to be abolished and replaced by land attachment.

Land attachment

Land attachment is really just adjudication, reformed (just as 'attachment' is poinding, reformed). Legislators like to get rid of terminology that sounds old-fashioned. The procedure is simpler than for adjudication and so land attachment may be more widely used. The procedure begins with the registration of a notice in both the Land Register (or Sasine Register) and the Register of Inhibitions. There are protections where the property is the debtor's home.

Landlord's hypothec

The Bill abolishes the landlord's hypothec for all moveables 'kept in a dwellinghouse, on agricultural land or on a croft'. It survives for leases of commercial property. (The hypothec is already inapplicable to most agricultural leases because of the Hypothec Abolition (Scotland) Act 1880, which Act is repealed by the Bill.) Sequestration for rent is also abolished, so that the benefit of the hypothec – in such cases where it still exists – emerges only in the course of some other proceeding, such as liquidation.

Planning (Scotland) Bill

The Planning (Scotland) Bill was introduced to the Scottish Parliament on 19 December 2005. If enacted, it will not replace the Town and County Planning (Scotland) Act 1997, but will amend it extensively.

Perhaps the most significant development from a conveyancing standpoint is the repeal and replacement of s 75 of the 1997 Act. Section 75 agreements (or s 50 agreements as they were under the earlier legislation) are agreements which can be entered into between an owner (in practice a developer) and the planning authority, and which, on being registered in the Land Register or Register of Sasines, bind not only the owner but also singular successors. The new Bill keeps the general idea but extends it in a number of ways, and also updates some of the provisions in the light of the Title Conditions (Scotland) Act 2003. One significant change is that whereas under existing law s 75 agreements are bilateral agreements between the owner and the planning authority, the Bill also allows (as an option) a unilateral grant by the owner. This necessitates a change of terminology, and accordingly the Bill replaces the term 'planning agreement' by 'planning obligation'. The requirement of registration will, of course, remain.

Another noteworthy change is the introduction of 'good neighbour agreements' (GNAs). This, we are told, is all about 'empowering communities': see the Bill's Policy Memorandum para 182. These GNAs are rather like ordinary planning agreements. But whereas planning agreements (or planning obligations) are enforceable by the planning authority, GNAs are enforceable by either (i) the community council, or (ii) a local amenity association. Like planning agreements (or obligations), they will be registered, and enforceable against singular successors. As with planning agreements, developers are not compelled to enter into GNAs. One technical issue is whether the 'community body' which is the counterparty in a GNA can be a voluntary unincorporated association. The issue is important because many amenity bodies have that status. The Bill is silent. If the Bill is passed without clarification on this point, we would suggest that those who are involved in GNAs should ensure that the amenity association is either (i) incorporated (eg as a company limited by guarantee) or (ii) a trust.

Investigation by Ombudsman: compulsory purchase

Mr C complained to the Scottish Ombudsman about maladministration by the Scottish Executive's responsible department, the strangely-named Enterprise Transport & Lifelong Learning Department. Land had been compulsorily purchased from him for development of the A74. His complaints were that the Department had failed to:

(a) clarify responsibility for future maintenance work on a private water main to the estate, which crosses the motorway;
(b) identify the location of another water pipe for which he is responsible;
(c) conclude a legal agreement about the use of shared access;
(d) return land that was compulsorily purchased and not used; and
(e) respond to correspondence.

All five complaints were upheld by the Ombudsman, Professor Alice Brown. (As a point of administrative law, the Scottish Parliamentary Commissioner for Administration was replaced by the Scottish Ombudsman under the provisions of the Scottish Public Services Ombudsman Act 2002.) The Ombudsman's report, issued on 22 July 2005, can be found at www.scottishombudsman.org.uk/cases_reports/assets/report22jul.doc.

Upset prices

In an important ruling, given on 19 January 2005, the Advertising Standards Authority decided that to advertise a property at a price lower than the expected sale price, as is normal in Scotland, was not to advertise in a misleading way. Its adjudication was as follows (see www.asa.org.uk/asa/adjudications):

> The advertisers believed the 'offers over' price for the house was not set artificially low; they said it was not standard practice in the United Kingdom to have an independent valuation of a property before marketing. They argued that, in Scotland, it was standard practice to market a property with an 'offers over' asking price, known as the 'upset price', that would encourage consumers to view the property and stimulate multiple offers to help reach the price the seller hoped to achieve. The advertisers said consumers placed their offers through property solicitors or advisers, who used their market knowledge to advise them on what price should be offered to secure the property; they asserted that most consumers would not have a property surveyed before bidding. The advertisers maintained that, to decide the 'upset price' for the property in the advertisement, they had reviewed the asking, and sale, prices of other properties in the area and those in similar areas. They said they had taken into account that the house needed modernisation, was on a busy main road and was too far from Edinburgh to be suitable for a daily commuter.
>
> The Authority noted the system of sealed bids used in the Scottish property market and noted most prospective buyers would receive advice on the sum they should offer to secure the property. It considered that Scottish property buyers, familiar with the Scottish property market and its use of sealed bids, would expect an 'offers over' price to be significantly lower than the eventual selling price. It concluded that, because the 'offers over' price was a minimum price for sale, readers would be likely to view it as similar to the reserve price in an auction and were unlikely to believe the property could be secured for that price in an open market. The Authority concluded that the advertisement was therefore unlikely to mislead.

Gazumping

Gazumping is the subject of a new Law Society Guideline:

> Where a solicitor for a seller has intimated verbally or in writing to the solicitors for a prospective purchaser that their client's offer is acceptable – whether after a closing date or otherwise – the seller's solicitor should not accept subsequent instructions from the seller to accept an offer from another party unless or until negotiations with the original offeror have fallen through. The solicitor should advise the seller to instruct another solicitor if he wishes to accept the later offer.
>
> This Guideline extends the Guideline on Closing Dates [1999, paras 3 and 4: see *Parliament House Book* p F1222 or www.lawscot.org.uk] to a situation where no closing date has been fixed.

Gazundering

Gazundering is likewise the subject of a new Law Society Guideline:

> Solicitors acting for prospective purchasers of residential property should advise their clients that if their offer is accepted – either verbally or in writing – the solicitors will require to withdraw from acting if the client subsequently wishes to renegotiate the price downwards without a valid reason arising out of an unforeseen problem with

the title or the condition of the property. Where an offer has been submitted subject to survey, and the survey discloses a problem – eg unauthorised alterations; new windows; damp or rot requiring specialist treatment – the solicitors would be entitled to accept instructions to seek to adjust the price in the light of that problem. However if the survey discloses no such problem but the valuation is regarded as too low by the offeror, solicitors should not accept instructions to withdraw the original offer and re-submit a lower offer but should refer the client to other solicitors if the client insists on doing so.

Purchasers' solicitors should advise the clients in advance of submitting an offer that if the client subsequently wishes to re-negotiate the price downwards without good reason, the solicitor will require to withdraw from acting.

There is no difficulty where the seller initiates renegotiation at a lower price if the prospective purchaser has withdrawn an offer due to an unsatisfactory survey, whether or not valuation was the sole issue.

This and the previous Guideline have been criticised. Writing in the April issue of the *Journal of the Law Society of Scotland* (p 10), Graeme McCormick asked why the Guidelines should attempt to innovate on the legal position, which is that parties are not bound until missives are concluded:

These Guidelines are presumably designed to impose a moral sanction on wayward punters. With one or two exceptions the reaction will be that they will just go to another solicitor who will earn his/her crust from a client's immorality while denying the previous solicitor his/her fee.

In the February issue of the *Journal* (p 51), James Ness, writing on behalf of the Professional Practice Committee, defended the Guideline on Gazundering as being directed at 'purchasers who put in unrealistically high offers with a view to eliminating the competition and then seek to take advantage of their status as preferred bidders to renegotiate the price down'. Responding to concerns expressed (at p 50) by Struan Douglas about the application of the Guideline to subject-to-survey offers where, following a lower-than-expected valuation, purchasers may wish to lower the price, Mr Ness said that:

In the Committee's view the seller is entitled to know if valuation is critical to the offer, and if that is the case it should be stated. For example a clause might state that the offer is not only subject to survey but also to the valuation in that survey being sufficient to support the loan required by the purchaser. Clearly, this puts the seller on notice as to the real terms of the suspensive condition and they can factor that into their decision as to whether or not to accept the offer.

If such a clause is not used, a purchaser who is unhappy with the valuation must simply withdraw – or instruct new agents. But there is no objection if the *seller*, faced with such a withdrawal, then proposes a reduction in the price.

Cancelling or changing a closing date

The current Law Society Guideline on Closing Dates and Notes of Interest dates from 1999. See www.lawscot.org.uk or *Parliament House Book* p F1222. As para 1 of that Guideline makes clear, '[t]here is no legal requirement on a selling solicitor to fix a closing date when more than one interest is noted'. Assuming, however, that a closing date is duly fixed, a new Guideline now provides that it should not be cancelled:

> Where a client has instructed a solicitor to intimate a closing date to other solicitors who have noted interest, that solicitor should withdraw from acting if the selling client wishes to cancel the closing date and accept an offer submitted in advance of it. Sellers' solicitors should therefore advise their clients of this in advance of fixing a closing date.

But a closing date can be changed if those who have noted interest are informed and, in a case where the date is brought forward, are given reasonable notice of the new date: see (2005) 50 *Journal of the Law Society of Scotland* February/51.

E-missives and standard missives

A new initiative to adjust missives electronically is launched and described at www.e-missives.co.uk. The website also helpfully reproduces the text of a number of regional standard offers (Aberdeen, Edinburgh, Glasgow and Highland) and subjects them to a detailed comparison. For a general discussion of standard missives, see an article by Peter Nicholson at (2005) 50 *Journal of the Law Society of Scotland* June/20.

Styles for deeds involving servitudes and real burdens

The Property Standardisation Group has produced styles for the main deeds which create real burdens and servitudes. These are deeds of conditions, deeds of servitudes, deeds of real burdens (three styles) and dispositions (two styles). A guide is provided by Ann E A Stewart at (2005) 50 *Journal of the Law Society of Scotland* August/56 and September/50. The styles themselves can be downloaded from www.psglegal.co.uk.

Style for certificate of title

The Property Standardisation Group has produced a style certificate of title, modelled on the City of London Law Society Certificate (5th edn). It is available for downloading at www.psglegal.co.uk. A guide is provided by Iain Macniven at (2005) 50 *Journal of the Law Society of Scotland* Nov/56.

FSA and mortgage activities

Mortgage lending came under the regulatory supervision of the Financial Services Authority in 2004. Some lenders have, it seems, been unaware that law firms that do not have direct authorisation with the FSA can nevertheless undertake some types of business in terms of the Law Society of Scotland's Incidental Financial Business (IFB) regime. Steps have been taken to make the position clear to lenders. See (2005) 50 *Journal of the Law Society of Scotland* Feb/38 and April/10.

Solicitors (Scotland) (Client Communication) Practice Rules 2005

The Solicitors (Scotland) (Client Communication) Practice Rules 2005 were approved at the Law Society AGM (which is advisory to rather than binding on the Council as respects practice rules) in March 2005. But this approval was subject to an amendment to rule 6 to the effect that breach of the Rules should be treated as inadequate professional service rather than professional misconduct. For different points of view on this topic see (2005) 50 *Journal of the Law Society of Scotland* April/11 and 33, and June/11. When the draft Rules as amended were submitted to the Lord President, he asked the Society to reinstate the original wording of rule 6, on the basis that s 34(4) of the Solicitors (Scotland) Act 1980 provides in any event that breach of a practice rule may be treated as misconduct. At its meeting on 1 July the Council decided to make the Rules in their original form. They came into force on 1 August 2005.

Under the Rules solicitors are required to provide information in writing to clients about certain matters. In relation to conveyancing transactions the matters are:

- details of the work to be done;
- an estimate of the total fee (including VAT and outlays) or the basis upon which the fee will be charged (including VAT and outlays);
- who will do the work;
- who the client should contact if there is concern about the way in which the work is being carried out.

With certain exceptions, this information must be provided at the earliest practicable opportunity upon receiving instructions. Typically, but not necessarily, the information will be given in a single letter.

The Professional Practice Committee has waived the requirement to provide written information to mortgage lenders in domestic conveyancing transactions where solicitors are acting for both lender and borrower. This is because lenders already set out the terms of the relationship in their instructions to solicitors, and the fees are paid by the borrower. See (2005) 50 *Journal of the Law Society of Scotland* Nov/38.

Money laundering

The Proceeds of Crime Act 2002 s 328 provides that 'a person commits an offence if he enters into or becomes concerned in an arrangement which he knows or suspects facilitates (by whatever means) the acquisition, retention, use or control of criminal property by or on behalf of another person ...'. Property is 'criminal property' if 'it constitutes a person's benefit from criminal conduct or it represents such a benefit (in whole or part and whether directly or indirectly)' (s 340). In *Conveyancing 2003* pp 34–36 we discussed the English case of *P v P* [2004] Fam 1, [2003] 4 All ER 843, which dealt with s 328. That decision has now been overruled by the Court of Appeal: *Bowman v Fels* [2005] EWCA Civ 226, [2005] 1 WLR 3083. In substance the decision says that s 328 does not affect the conduct of litigation by legal professionals. The case contains strong dicta about the sanctity of legal professional privilege, but to what extent these dicta might be extended to conveyancing is a matter for speculation. See further Bruce Ritchie, 'Drawing the line' (2005) 50 *Journal of the Law Society of Scotland* April/38; Ken Swinton, 'Money Laundering and POCA' (2005) 73 *Scottish Law Gazette* 65.

Registers of Scotland

ARTL

It remains the intention to introduce Automated Registration of Title to Land (ARTL) in late 2006. Before this can be done it will be necessary to amend some primary legislation (principally the Requirements of Writing (Scotland) Act 1995) by a statutory instrument made under s 8 of the Electronic Communications Act 2000. A draft statutory instrument was published for consultation in 2005. ARTL will be available for dealings in whole but not for first registrations, and will be optional.

Feudal abolition etc: updating of title sheets

The Keeper is embarking on an ambitious programme in which he will update the one million or so title sheets that have so far been created to take account of the extinction of superiors' rights and the abolition of the common law rules of implied enforcement rights for real burdens. This will involve the deletion of burdens and, in appropriate cases, the making of a statement, under s 58 of the Title Conditions (Scotland) Act 2003, as to the existence and extent of implied enforcement rights under ss 52 to 56 of the Act. The Keeper will also remove any reference to non-leasehold irritancy, to feuduty (except where it defines apportionment of maintenance obligations), to expired manager burdens, and to the School Sites Act 1841. See Registers of Scotland, *Update 10.6* (available on www.ros.gov.uk/updates).

An initial pilot has been taking place for East Lothian. The intention is to complete all counties over the next 10 years according to a timetable which will be made public. Once a title sheet has been updated it will contain the following note, at the end of the burdens (D) section:

> Where the Keeper considers that any real burdens which affected the subjects in this title were extinguished by virtue of s 17 of the Abolition of Feudal Tenure etc (Scotland) Act 2000 and s 49 of the Title Conditions (Scotland) Act 2003, these have been removed or omitted from the title sheet. Further, where the Keeper is satisfied that any remaining real burdens subsist by virtue of the rights of enforcement constituted by s 60 of the

said Act of 2000 or ss 52 to 54 and s 56 of the said Act of 2003, a statement or statements to that effect have also been entered.

Notices of potential liability for costs

Notices of potential liability for costs can be registered in respect of common repairs, most notably in tenements. The effect is that, if the work has been carried out but not yet paid for, a new owner of the flat or house against which the notice is registered will be liable for the relevant share of the cost. See the Title Conditions (Scotland) Act 2003 s 10A and the Tenements (Scotland) Act 2004 s 13, discussed in *Conveyancing 2004* pp 141–142. Further guidance on registration matters in respect of such notices is given in Registers of Scotland, *Update 14* (available on www.ros.gov.uk/updates).

Practice Book online

The *Registration of Title Practice Book* is now available online, at www.ros.gov.uk/rotbook, and is fully searchable. This is the second edition, of 2000. There are no immediate plans to keep it up to date.

Payment of fees by variable direct debit

Since 31 October 2005 it has been possible to pay registration fees by (variable) direct debit rather than by cheque. The key advantage of doing so is to avoid the risk of an application being rejected because of non-payment or payment of the wrong amount. Direct debit will also be needed for ARTL transactions. The Guarantee Committee of the Law Society has issued guidance to the effect that the principal client account should not be subject to variable direct debits, and that a separate account should be opened instead. For further details about variable direct debit, see Registers of Scotland, *Update 17* (available on www.ros.gov.uk/updates).

Redemption money for feuduty: last chance

All remaining feuduties were abolished, with abolition of the feudal system, on 28 November 2004. But in terms of part 3 of the Abolition of Feudal Tenure etc (Scotland) Act 2000 a former superior is entitled to redemption money. The money, however, must be claimed, by service of an appropriate notice, by 27 November 2006 at latest. For an account of the procedure, see K G C Reid, *The Abolition of Feudal Tenure in Scotland* (2003) ch 10.

Stamp duty land tax

New online facility

After a false start, a new system for submitting SDLT returns online was introduced on 26 August 2005. A note in the *Journal of the Law Society of Scotland* for September 2005 (p 52) summarises the procedure:

To use online submission, your firm must first register as an online user. Go to https: // online.inlandrevenue.gov.uk / index.jsp and click Register, choose to register as an agent, then on the next screen select Stamp Taxes Online. You will need to provide your firm's partnership unique taxpayer reference (or self assessment unique taxpayer reference if you are a sole trader). You will be given a stamp taxes online reference number (STORN). A user ID and activation PIN will be sent to you within seven days. Once you have activated your registration, you can set up assistants who will each be given a user ID and must choose a password. Assistants can then log in at the link above and start preparing returns.

Unlike the existing internet print and post service, online submission can be used for linked transactions, and for a maximum of 99 purchasers, vendors or pieces of land. In most cases the system calculates the SDLT, although for linked transactions you have to calculate the SDLT yourself. Similarly, the system does not calculate the net present value of leases, which has to be inserted.

The online submission software is more sophisticated than the print and post version, as it only asks you to complete those parts of the return which are relevant to your transaction, and also makes sure that all relevant details have been provided. There are extensive validation checks also, which ensure that the return once submitted will be accepted.

You do not need a return number (UTRN) to start off a return – the UTRN is generated only when the return has been submitted. You will need 'blank payslips' which have no UTRN on them. Once the return has been submitted and you have received the UTRN, this must be written on the payslip and sent to Netherton with the payment. Payment can be made by cheque as before.

The client must approve the content of the return before it is submitted. You can either ask the client to approve all of the contents of the return, or alternatively all of the contents of the return apart from the effective date. A copy in return format can be sent to the client for signature. The declaration on this version is as follows:

'The information contained in this copy of the return is correct and complete to the best of my knowledge and belief. I authorise my agent to submit a return, containing this information, electronically on my behalf. If the information I have approved does not include the effective date, I also authorise my agent to enter the effective date in the return on my behalf.'

If the client is asked to approve all of the return except the effective date, the practitioner inserts the effective date before submitting the return. This means that you can prepare the return (apart from the effective date) in advance of settlement, arrange for the client to approve it, and then at settlement insert the effective date and submit the return.

On submission of the return you will receive a submission receipt, and you should keep a copy of this.

The actual certificate continues to be issued in paper form. For further details, see an article by Iain Doran and Danny Freedman published on p 60 of the *Journal of the Law Society of Scotland* for March 2005.

Personal presentation in Edinburgh

Some alterations have been made to the system of personal presentation in Edinburgh in order to take account of electronic submission. The original statement as to when and how personal presentation can be used can be found in *Conveyancing 2003* pp 148–149. Typically it is available in corporate transactions where the letter of obligation does not extend to the charges register and the company file.

The changes are as follows:

The solicitor wishing to present personally must complete the attached declaration setting out why the 'same day' service is required. This should be presented in person to the Edinburgh Stamp Office within two working days of the effective date of the transaction together with:

in the case of a paper return:

- the completed form SDLT 1 (and any supplementary returns required) and
- payment (or evidence thereof)

or

in the case of e-submission:

- a printed PDF (PDF black and white version of SDLT1) from the e channel and
- the print of the submission receipt and UTRN.

In e-submission cases you have 30 days to pay so there is no need to pay at the counter and payment should be made as if it was a normal e-submission case.

Agents should note to file and keep the automatic certificate (second cert) when received in their files for record purposes.

Assuming that the returns are in order, the Edinburgh Stamp office will give the solicitor a handwritten SDLT certificate.

The date on which the land transaction return was presented to the Edinburgh Stamp Office counts as the date on which the transaction was notified to the Inland Revenue.

The SDLT certificate can then be taken to the Registers with the documents so that registration can take place.

The Edinburgh Stamp Office will send the land transaction return(s) to Netherton and they will be processed in the usual manner.

The declaration is in the following terms:

DECLARATION IN RESPECT OF SPECIAL ARRANGEMENTS FOR PERSONAL PRESENTATION IN EDINBURGH

Name and address of solicitor

Unique reference number of SDLT 1

I confirm that the land transaction return with the above unique reference falls within the Special Arrangements criteria agreed between the Inland Revenue and the Law Society of Scotland as detailed below and that registration within two working days after the effective date is required.

Please tick a box to indicate which applies	
	(1) the seller is a corporate entity and the seller's solicitor has not given a solicitor's personal letter of obligation in respect of the charges register and the company file, or
	(2) the seller's solicitor has been requested to give a solicitor's personal letter of obligation but has refused to do so, or
	(3) the purchaser needs to register ownership on or before obtaining access to the transaction funding

Signed ....

16 days and still no SDLT certificate

If, despite a return having been made promptly, an SDLT certificate has not arrived 16 days after the 'effective date of the transaction' (ie settlement), it is now possible to obtain a handwritten certificate by applying by fax to the Edinburgh Stamp Office. The fax number is 0131 442 3038.

SDLT returns: some hints

Ten handy hints for submission of SDLT returns have been drawn up by the Law Society's Tax Law Committee. They are reproduced at p 61 of the March 2005 issue of the *Journal of the Law Society of Scotland*.

Minutes of waiver etc

Minutes of waiver require a self-certificate (or, if the consideration exceeds £60,000, an ordinary SDLT certificate). The rule is the same for variations and discharges of community burdens under ss 33 and 35 of the Title Conditions (Scotland) Act

2003. On the other hand a certificate is not needed for notices of termination (s 20), notices of preservation (s 50), and notices of converted servitude (s 80). See (2005) 50 *Journal of the Law Society of Scotland* Jan/48.

Changes in the law: Finance Act 2005 and Finance (No 2) Act 2005

For an account of the changes introduced by the Finance Act 2005 and the Finace (No 2) Act 2005, see p 141.

Reform of land registration

In 2005 the Scottish Law Commission published two discussion papers on land registration: *Land Registration: Registration, Rectification and Indemnity* (Scot Law Com DP No 128) and *Land Registration: Miscellaneous Issues* (Scot Law Com DP No 130). Both are available on www.scotlawcom.gov.uk. They build on proposals set out in an earlier discussion paper, *Land Registration: Void and Voidable Titles* (Scot Law Com DP No 125) published in 2004: see *Conveyancing 2004* pp 50–51. The consultation period closes on 31 March 2006. For a discussion, see (2006) 51 *Journal of the Law Society of Scotland* Feb/48.

Taken together, these three papers propose widespread changes in the law – but not necessarily the practice – of registration of title. As under the current legislation, a *bona fide* acquirer will be able to rely on the Land Register – a principle which the Law Commission calls the 'integrity principle'. So if the Register shows the owner to be A whereas the true owner is in fact B, a purchaser is free to acquire from A and will receive a good title. But for the integrity principle to operate there must also have been possession of the property for a certain period (such as one year) either by the transferor or by the acquirer. If the acquirer's own deed is invalid for some reason (for example, an error in expression, or a forged or faulty signature) the acquirer's title will also not be good. This is because registration will no longer, of itself, confer a good title. Instead the acquirer will be entitled to indemnity (assuming good faith) and the true owner will keep the property. The idea is that the new legislation should favour acquirers slightly less and existing owners slightly more – or, in other words, that it should make titles on the Land Register more secure than they are at present.

The discussion papers are highly critical of the Land Registration (Scotland) Act 1979 and propose its replacement by legislation which is clearer, more rationally based, and properly integrated with the general law of property. The papers also contain detailed proposals on matters such as rectification, indemnity, descriptions, and servitudes and other overriding interests.

Conflict of interest

Hilton v Barker Booth & Eastwood [2005] UKHL 8, [2005] 1 WLR 567 is an important English House of Lords case on conflict of interest. In 1990 Hilton contracted to sell property to Bromage with a view to redevelopment. The deal was a complex one and involved a significant amount of money. Messrs Barker Booth & Eastwood acted for both parties. What they knew, and Hilton did not, was that Bromage had a criminal record for fraud. They did not tell Hilton. Had Hilton had that information he would not have entered into the contract with Bromage. When the date of completion arrived Bromage failed to pay the price. Hilton lost a great deal of money. As long ago as 1993 he raised the present action for damages against the defendants. He lost at first instance and again in the Court of Appeal. The reasoning was that if he had been represented by other solicitors it is unlikely that they would have known of Bromage's history, and so the fact that he had retained Messrs Barker Booth & Eastwood had not in fact harmed him. The House of Lords, reversing the Court of Appeal, found the defendants liable. The defendants did know of Bromage's past and therefore had a duty to disclose it. The fact that they also may have had a duty to Bromage to conceal that history did not alter the fact that they were in breach of the obligations to Hilton. If they found themselves in an impossible position they had only themselves to blame for having chosen to act for both parties.

Acting for both buyer and seller, once not uncommon, has now disappeared, apart from certain exceptional cases. But it must be borne in mind that solicitors still do often act for two parties whose interests may not turn out to be the same. Thus they commonly act for both debtor and creditor in residential loans. They often act for both husband and wife, or for both partners. In all such cases there is a risk of conflict of interest.

Books

D L Carey Miller with David Irvine, *Corporeal Moveables in Scots Law* (Thomson W Green 2005; ISBN 0 414 01400 6)

George Jamieson, *Family Law Agreements* (Tottel Publishing 2005; ISBN 1 845 92004 X)

Kenneth G C Reid and George L Gretton, *Conveyancing 2004* (Avizandum Publishing Ltd 2005; ISBN 1 904968 01 5)

Robert Rennie, *Land Tenure and Tenements Legislation* (2nd edn) (Thomson W Green 2005; ISBN 0 414 01613 0)

Articles

James Aitken, 'SDLT: getting it right' (2005) *Journal of the Law Society of Scotland* July/56

A D Anderson, 'Building standards assessments – replacing letters of comfort' (2005) 73 *Scottish Law Gazette* 12

Ross Gilbert Anderson, '"Offside goals" before *Rodger Builders*' 2005 *Juridical Review* 277

Stuart Bain, 'Still thumbs down' (2005) 50 *Journal of the Law Society of Scotland* Nov/52 (making the arguments against the single survey)

Alan Barr, 'The anti-avoidance device' (2005) 50 *Journal of the Law Society of Scotland* Aug/19 (considering budget changes in SDLT)

David Bone, 'A blow for the future' (2005) 50 *Journal of the Law Society of Scotland* July/26 and Sept/22 (considering wind farms)

Stewart Brymer, 'Thinking of buying or selling a home – think single survey?' (2005) 74 *Greens Property Law Bulletin* 1

Stewart Brymer, 'Thin edge of the wedge?' (2005) 50 *Journal of the Law Society of Scotland* April/50 (considering the single survey)

Stewart Brymer, 'The future of the Scottish missive' (2005) 75 *Greens Property Law Bulletin* 1

Stewart Brymer, 'ARTL: the current state of play' (2005) 76 *Greens Property Law Bulletin* 4

Stewart Brymer, 'The purchaser information pack: fact or fiction?' (2005) 78 *Greens Property Law Bulletin* 1

Stewart Brymer, George Gretton, Roderick Paisley and Robert Rennie, 'Opinion prepared for the Keeper of the Registers of Scotland: automated registration of title to land' 2005 *Juridical Review* 201

Graham Burnside, 'Unveiling the Islamic mortgage' (2005) 50 *Journal of the Law Society of Scotland* Dec/58

David Cabrelli, 'The curious case of the "unreal" floating charge' 2005 SLT (News) 127 (considering the Enterprise Act 2002)

David Cabrelli, 'The case against the floating charge in Scotland' (2005) 9 *Edinburgh Law Review* 407

Joel Conn, 'Mortgage Rights (Scotland) Act 2001: three years on' (2005) 62 *Greens Civil Practice Bulletin* 2

Lorne Crerar, 'The single survey: why it should be supported' (2005) *Journal of the Law Society of Scotland* Sept/46

Mike Dailly, 'Expenses in mortgage repossession cases' (2004) 60 *Greens Civil Practice Bulletin* 6

Peter Drummond-Murray of Mastrick, 'Baronial Heraldic Additaments' 2005 SLT (News) 161

Tom Drysdale, 'ARTL – an interim report' (2005) 73 *Scottish Law Gazette* 124

Tim Edward and Alistair Sim, 'Know your boundaries' (2005) 50 *Journal of the Law Society of Scotland* Oct/32 (considering the risk management aspects of boundary disputes)

Ian C Ferguson, 'Practical implications of the appointed day' (2005) 73 *Scottish Law Gazette* 18

Ian C Ferguson, 'Don't make it compulsory' (2005) 50 *Journal of the Law Society of Scotland* June/54 (opposing plans to introduce the single survey)

Alasdair G Fox, 'Let the access taker beware' (2005) 50 *Journal of the Law Society of Scotland* March/55 (considering occupier's liability in respect of access taken under part 1 of the Land Reform (Scotland) Act 2003)

Alasdair G Fox, 'Rise and rise of the Land Court' (2005) 50 *Journal of the Law Society of Scotland* June/48 (considering the Land Court's new jurisdiction under part 7 of the Agricultural Holdings (Scotland) Act 2003)

Alasdair G Fox, 'A right and its exercise' (2005) 50 *Journal of the Law Society of Scotland* Sept/40 (considering the landlord's position in relation to the tenant's right to buy under part 2 of the Agricultural Holdings (Scotland) Act 2003)

Alasdair G Fox, 'The limits of diversification' (2005) 50 *Journal of the Law Society of Scotland* Dec/52 (considering *Trustees of the Cawdor Scottish Discretionary Trust v Mackay* 12 September 2005, Scottish Land Court)

Graham Gibson, 'ARTL – an opportunity to make conveyancing more profitable' (2005) 75 *Greens Property Law Bulletin* 3

Ian Gray, 'Flooding investigation' (2005) 75 *Greens Property Law Bulletin* 6

George Gretton, 'Insolvency risk in sale' 2005 *Juridical Review* 335

John A Lovett, 'A new way: servitude relocation in Scotland and Louisiana' (2005) 9 *Edinburgh Law Review* 352

Iain Macniven, 'Money laundering for property lawyers' (2005) 76 *Greens Property Law Bulletin* 6

Donna McKenzie Skene, 'Whose estate is it anyway? The debtor's estate on sequestration' 2005 *Juridical Review* 311

Laura Marcantonio, 'Exchanging the "missive"' (2005) 50 *Journal of the Law Society of Scotland* Oct/11 (considering standard-form contracts in Queensland)

Peter Nicholson, 'Buying in quick deals' (2005) 50 *Journal of the Law Society of Scotland* June/20 (considering standard missives)

Roderick Paisley, 'Personal real burdens' 2005 *Juridical Review* 377

Roderick Paisley, 'Real rights: practical problems and dogmatic rigidity' (2005) 9 *Edinburgh Law Review* 267

Christopher Rae, 'Building Regulations – May 2005' (2005) 77 *Greens Property Law Bulletin* 5

Colin T Reid and Derek J McGlashan, 'Erosion, Accretion and Intervention' 2005 *Juridical Review* 73

Donald Reid, 'Fair notice?' (2005) 50 *Journal of the Law Society of Scotland* Jan/44 (considering notices of potential liability for cost under s 13 of the Tenements (Scotland) Act 2004)

Robert Rennie, 'Control of land in the post-feudal era' 2005 SLT (News) 89

Robert Rennie, 'The race to the Registers revisited' (2005) 50 *Journal of the Law Society of Scotland* July/53

Bruce Ritchie, 'Drawing the line' (2005) 50 *Journal of the Law Society of Scotland* April/38 (considering *Bowman v Fels* [2005] EWCA Civ 226, [2005] 1 WLR 3083)

Fiona Rollo, 'Licences to occupy: can solicitors do more than constitute in writing what could amount to a licence?' (2005) 78 *Greens Property Law Bulletin* 3

Kenneth Ross, 'What a waste!' (2005) 50 *Journal of the Law Society of Scotland* May/54 (considering *Van de Walle v Texaco Belgium SA*, ECJ, 7 September 2004)

Charles Sandison, 'Don't fall at the final hurdle' (2005) 50 *Journal of the Law Society of Scotland* Nov/34 (considering post-completion matters from the perspective of risk management)

Charles Sandison and David Williamson, 'Environmental liabilities in transactions' (2005) 76 *Greens Property Law Bulletin* 1

Andrew J M Steven, 'Property law and human rights' 2005 *Juridical Review* 293

Andrew J M Steven, 'Title conditions: servitudes and real burdens compared' (2005) 73 *Scottish Law Gazette* 81

Nicola Stewart, 'Litigation possibilities and the Title Conditions (Scotland) Act 2003' (2005) 62 *Greens Civil Practice Bulletin* 6 (considering the Lands Tribunal jurisdiction)

Ken Swinton, 'Self granted a non domino dispositions' (2005) 73 *Scottish Law Gazette* 52 (considering *Board of Management of Aberdeen College v Youngson* 2005 SC 335)

Ken Swinton, 'Little Red Riding Hood and Goldilocks hit the road: endowment mis-selling' (2005) 73 *Scottish Law Gazette* 57

Ken Swinton, 'Money Laundering and POCA' (2005) 73 *Scottish Law Gazette* 65

Ken Swinton, 'Parking again: *Moncrieff v Jamieson* 2005 CSIH 14' (2005) 73 *Scottish Law Gazette* 96

Ken Swinton, 'Prescription, human rights and bijuralism' (considering *Beaulane Properties Ltd v Palmer* [2005] 3 WLR 554)

Ken Swinton, 'Prescription, human rights and the Land Register: *Pye v UK*' (2005) 73 *Scottish Law Gazette* 179

Richard Turnbull, 'The Tenancy of Shops (Scotland) Act 1949 – time for renewal?' (2005) 79 *Greens Property Law Bulletin* 3

Scott Wortley, 'Love thy neighbour: the development of the Scottish law of implied third-party rights of enforcement of real burdens' 2005 *Juridical Review* 345

❧ PART IV ❧
COMMENTARY

COMMENTARY

MISSIVES OF SALE

Rescission for non-payment: how?

Missives commonly provide that, if the price remains unpaid for a stipulated period (such as 14 days) after the contractual date of entry, the seller can rescind the contract 'on giving prior written notice to that effect' to the buyer. The practical question of how, precisely, notice is to be given was considered in *Miller v Maguire*.[1]

The first issue was *when* such notice can be given. In *Miller* the date of entry was 6 December 2003, and the alleged notice was sent on 11 December 2003, ie before the expiry of the 14-day period. Was this too early? In the opinion of the sheriff,[2] it was not too early.

The second issue was more difficult. Did the letter of 11 December, from the sellers' solicitors, amount to a written notice of rescission? The relevant passage from the letter was as follows:

> Given your client's failure to pay the price on the date of entry specified in the missives, namely 6 December, 2003 our clients reserve the right to charge interest on the price and to exercise the other rights competent to them in terms of the missives.

The sheriff took the view that this could be read as requisite notice. The opposite view seems more convincing. A contract continues to exist until the right of rescission has been actually exercised.[3] It is difficult to read this letter as exercising such a right. Indeed, it seems to be saying the exact opposite, by warning the buyer that the right might be exercised at a future date.[4]

Rescission for non-payment: how much?

Assuming that proper notice is given, and the contract is validly rescinded, the next question is entitlement to damages. This was the question considered in *Kerr v McCormack*.[5]

---

1 10 August 2005, Glasgow Sheriff Court, A322/04.
2 Sheriff C A L Scott.
3 Cf *Cumming v Brown* 1993 SCLR 707 and *Grovebury Management Ltd v McLaren* 1997 SLT 1083. To this general rule there are exceptions.
4 In fact there was a second letter, on 23 December 2003, which may have made things clearer.
5 12 January 2005, Glasgow Sheriff Court, A1300/04.

Missives were concluded for the sale of a house in Pollokshields in Glasgow at the price of £875,000. When the buyer did not pay, the sellers rescinded (as was their right under missives) and put the house back on the market. It was sold for £950,000. This sale also fell through. The sellers rescinded and put the house back on the market again. The house was sold for a third time, this time successfully, at a lower price (£870,000). This was some seven months after the first sale. In this action the sellers sought damages against the first buyer. In particular they sought (i) interest on the unpaid price (£12,046.23),[1] and (ii) damages for certain other expenses such as storage and legal expenses (£11,108.59). No challenge was made to (i) but the buyer resisted (ii). His argument was simple. The provision in missives about interest was a liquidated damages clause, ie an agreement in advance between the parties as to how much was to be paid by way of damages in the event of default. Interest must thus be paid, as the parties had agreed, but no further sum was then due by way of damages.

The importance of the case is increased by the fact that the interest clause followed, almost word for word, a style published in the *Journal of the Law Society of Scotland* by Professor Rennie and Professor (now Sheriff) Cusine as long ago as 1993.[2] It is believed that the style is in common use.[3] The clause as it was used in *Kerr v McCormack* was as follows:[4]

[A] In the event of the purchase price or any part thereof remaining outstanding as at the date of entry, then notwithstanding consignation or the fact that entry has not been taken by your client [ie the buyer], your client shall be deemed to be in material breach of contract [B] and further, interest will accrue at the rate of 4 per centum per annum above Royal Bank of Scotland Base Lending Rate from time to time until full payment of the price is made, or in the event of our client [ie the sellers] exercising his option to rescind the contract, until the contractual date of entry of the first sale, [C] and further, interest shall run on any shortfall between the purchase price hereunder and the resale price until such shortfall shall have been paid to our client. [D] In the event that the said purchase price is not paid in full within 14 days of the date of entry our client shall be entitled to treat your client as being in material breach of contract and to rescind the Missives on giving prior written notice to that effect to your client [E] without prejudice to any rights or claims competent to our client arising from the breach of contract by your client including our client's rights to claim all losses, damages and expenses sustained as a result of your client's breach of contract including interest on the price calculated as set out in this clause and any bridging loan arrangement fee incurred by our client. [F] For the purpose of computation of our client's loss, the interest element of that loss shall be deemed to be a liquidated penalty provision exigible notwithstanding the exercise by our client of his option to rescind the contract

---

1 The judgment does not disclose the basis of this calculation, but it seems likely that the second abortive sale meant that the buyer under the first abortive sale was liable for interest only for a restricted period.

2 (1993) 38 *Journal of the Law Society of Scotland* 450. The style was a response to various decisions, most notably *Lloyds Bank plc v Bamberger* 1993 SC 570. For background see R Rennie, 'A matter of interest' (1993) 38 *Journal of the Law Society of Scotland* 363.

3 For other occasions on which this style has been judicially considered, see D J Cusine and R Rennie, *Missives* (2nd edn 1999) paras 8.21–8.31.

4 For ease of reference we have divided the passage into seven lettered parts, A–G.

for non-payment of the price or any repudiation of the contract by your client. [G] This clause shall have effect always provided that any unreasonable delay in settlement is not attributable to us or our clients.

The buyer's defence rested on part [F]. If the right to interest (set out in part [B]) was indeed 'a liquidated penalty provision', then it exhausted all other entitlement to damages. Accordingly, any claim for additional damages must fail. The sheriff[1] disagreed. In his view part [F] could be seen as distinguishing between the loss to the sellers in general and 'the interest element of that loss'. Only the latter was covered by the declaration as to a liquidated penalty provision. That interpretation was reinforced by part [E] of the clause, which made clear that the sellers were entitled *both* to interest and also to other damages. Accordingly, the sellers could claim both interest and also damages.

The sheriff's decision seems right. From a seller's point of view, three points at least seem worth making.

First – and regardless of whether the technical term is used – an interest clause is in the nature of a provision for liquidated damages. This is because the amount due does not turn on the seller's actual loss (which, depending on the circumstances, may be less) but rather is a pre-estimate of possible damages.[2] Unlike most such provisions, however, it relates only to one possible head of damage – for non-payment of the price – and is not intended to exclude claims in respect of other heads. It is important that the clause makes this clear. In the present case, the position was made clear by part [E] of the clause.

Secondly, it is not clear what is gained by a declaration that an interest provision amounts to liquidated damages. It seems positively to invite arguments of the kind which were made in *Kerr v McCormack.* Possibly the clause would be improved by the deletion of part [F]. One reason for using language of this kind is to emphasise that the provision is a pre-estimate of damages and not a penalty clause (which would not be enforced). But in matters of this kind, the label chosen by the parties is not conclusive.[3] Indeed, the words 'liquidated *penalty* provision' used in the clause are problematic, and arguably even contradictory.

Thirdly, if this case is anything to go by, the clause as originally proposed by Professors Rennie and Cusine has deteriorated in the course of repetition. In particular, the crucial words which finish part [B] do not make much sense. As given in *Kerr v McCormack* they provide that, in the event of rescission, interest will run 'until the contractual date of entry of the first sale'. But what is 'the first sale'? To say that it is the current – and now abortive – sale would be nonsensical; yet that is the natural meaning. The original version by Professors Rennie and Cusine is much clearer, with interest running 'until such time as our clients shall have completed a resale of the subjects and received the resale price'. As this

---

1 Sheriff John A Baird.
2 See generally H L MacQueen and J Thomson, *Contract Law in Scotland* (2000) paras 6.46–6.51; W W McBryde, *The Law of Contract in Scotland* (2nd edn 2001) paras 22-152–22-156.
3 *Dunlop Pneumatic Tyre Co Ltd v New Garage and Motor Co Ltd* [1915] AC 79 at 86 *per* Lord Dunedin.

example reminds us, when styles are being copied it is always necessary to be wary of the conveyancing equivalent of Chinese whispers.

Something should also be said about the buyer. From the buyer's perspective, clauses such as the one litigated in *Kerr v McCormack* are potentially oppressive. In the event of rescission, interest is to run, at a high rate, until a time which is partly of the seller's own choosing. If it takes months (or years) to resell the property, then interest must be paid for months (or years). If the seller's actual loss is much smaller, interest will still run at the stipulated rate. In our view, such an interest clause should not be accepted without qualification. It is noteworthy that in the various standard-form offers which have been winning local acceptance in recent years, interest is capped at a maximum of one year.[1] Even that is likely to be too generous to the seller: interest for a year at 4% above base (currently 4.5%) on the price paid in *Kerr v McCormack* (£875,000) would be £74,375.

Moreover, what happens if, far from making a loss, the seller makes a profit, because of a higher resale price? The general law says that the innocent party is entitled to damages that will compensate for *net* loss. Suppose the gross loss is £10,000 and the property is resold for £15,000 extra: there is no net loss and so the damages will be zero: *injuria sine damno*. Is the intention of part [F] to exclude abatement on account of profit? If so, it is not clearly stated, though arguably it is implied by the use of the word 'liquidated'. If this is the intention, it would be better to state it clearly, but in that case we suspect that few buyers would be willing to agree to it.

MMV: ANNUS MORTIS DOCTRINAE ACQUISITIONIS DOMINII RERUM IMMOBILIUM USUCAPIONE – FORTASSE

or

SO FAREWELL THEN, POSITIVE PRESCRIPTION?

Introduction

Positive prescription is something we all grew up with: an essential part of the conveyancing system. About the middle of the 1990s, the Keeper changed his policy about accepting *a non domino* dispositions and became much more reluctant to do so.[2] But the law remained as it was. In 2005 there have been three important cases. To speak of the 'death' of the doctrine, as we do above, is, indeed, premature, but in so far as the doctrine does survive it is likely to be in an attenuated form. In future it may be a marginal, not a central, doctrine in the conveyancing system.

---

1 See the regional offers set out at www.e-missives.co.uk.
2 A M Falconer and R Rennie, 'The Sasine Register and Dispositions *a non domino*' (1997) 42 *Journal of the Law Society of Scotland* 72. See also *Registration of Title Practice Book* para 6.4.

One of the three cases is Scottish: *Board of Management of Aberdeen College v Youngson*,[1] holding that a disposition in the form of A to A is not a good foundation writ for the purposes of positive prescription. Important though this decision is, its scope is limited. By contrast, *J A Pye (Oxford) Ltd v United Kingdom*[2] may possibly spell the end of the entire system, for the European Court of Human Rights held that the English equivalent of positive prescription, namely limitation, constitutes a violation of human rights where the title which is lost is a registered one, and that in any such case the UK Government must compensate for the loss. The third case is an English High Court decision, *Beaulane Properties Ltd v Palmer*,[3] in which the court found itself able to 'interpret' the legislation about limitation in such a way as to enable it to hold that title had not been lost.

News of the *Aberdeen College* case spread quickly, even before it had been reported. But the other two cases remain, so far, little known. Yet in the long run they may be the ones that will be remembered when *Aberdeen College* has become a mere footnote. But it is with that case that we begin.

Board of Management of Aberdeen College v Youngson

The case itself

By disposition dated 2 July 1993 and recorded GRS Aberdeen 23 July 1993, William, Gladys, Stewart and John Youngson disponed certain property to themselves. The disposition was *a non domino* (or rather *a non dominis*), for the property in fact belonged to Grampian Regional Council. About 1999 William and Gladys died, and their shares were transferred by docket to Stewart and John, the defenders in the action. Stewart and John did not complete title on the dockets. Thus at the time of the action each defender had a completed title to a quarter share and an uncompleted, docket, title to another quarter share. From 1993 onwards the Youngsons had possession of the land. Ten years elapsed before the title was challenged by the pursuer in the form of an action of reduction.

Section 1 of the Prescription and Limitation (Scotland) Act 1973 says that for positive prescription to run various requirements must be satisfied. One of them is that the foundation writ must be 'sufficient in respect of its terms to constitute in favour of that person a title to that interest in the particular land' and must not be 'invalid *ex facie*' or forged. The Lord Ordinary's view was that:[4]

> the disposition by William Phillip Youngson and others in favour of William Phillip Youngson and others recorded 23 July 1993 does not amount to a deed which is sufficient in respect of its terms to constitute in favour of the defenders a title to the interest in the subjects which they claim. I am also of the view that this disposition was a deed which is invalid *ex facie* for the purposes of s 1(1A) of the Prescription and Limitation (Scotland) Act 1973.

---

1 [2005] CSOH 31, 2005 SC 335, 2005 SLT 371.
2 15 November 2005, European Court of Human Rights.
3 [2005] 3 WLR 554.
4 Paragraph 14.

Hence, he concluded, the defenders' title had not been validated by positive prescription, and accordingly decree of reduction was pronounced.

General discussion

Is the decision right? The issue had not been previously considered by the courts. There had, however, been some academic discussion, which was duly placed before the court. We ourselves had expressed the view that it was 'somewhat doubtful' whether an A-to-A disposition can function as a foundation writ.[19] A different view is taken in the current edition of *Professor McDonald's Conveyancing Manual*, edited by David Brand, Andrew Steven and Scott Wortley.[2] Ken Swinton has argued that the decision is wrong.[3] Both Brand/Steven/Wortley and Swinton make valuable points, and there is certainly room for debate. We understand that the defenders did not reclaim. Given that the decision must raise questions about the validity of a significant number of titles, we would not be surprised if some other party were prepared to litigate the case up to the Inner House, seeking a different interpretation of the law.

It is important to note that the Lord Ordinary does not say that a disposition of the 'A to A' form could never be effective as a foundation writ. On this issue he reserves his opinion:[4]

> A person cannot dispone a piece of land from himself to himself in exactly the same status or category, because no transfer will have resulted. It may be different if the interest in land which is being disponed is different from that which is received, or where the capacity of the individual changes – for example, a person may dispone land to trustees of whose number he is one, or he may dispone land to a partnership of which he is a partner. In these examples the fact that the disponer's name appears both as disponer and amongst the disponees is neither here nor there, because his capacity is different and (at least in the example of the partnership) there is a separate legal persona involved.

It needs to be stressed that the *Aberdeen College* decision has no implications for the situation where prescription runs on an A-to-B disposition. Nor, it seems, does it affect cases where the Keeper has accepted (with exclusion of indemnity) an *a non domino* A-to-A disposition for registration in the Land Register, for in such a case prescription runs on the title sheet and not on the disposition.

Some implications

In the following three examples the story begins with an A-to-A *a non domino* disposition recorded in the Sasine Register. The first illustrates the Keeper's previous practice, while the second and third illustrate his practice since the *Aberdeen College* case was decided.

---

1 G L Gretton and K G C Reid, *Conveyancing* (3rd edn 2004) para 7-25.
2 7th edn 2004, para 12.7.
3 Ken Swinton, 'Self granted a non domino dispositions' (2005) 73 *Scottish Law Gazette* 52.
4 Paragraph 10.

(a) Jack's title is based on an *a non domino* Jack-to-Jack disposition re-corded in the Sasine Register in 1992. In 2003 Jack dispones to Jill. In 2003 the Keeper would have been prepared to register Jill in the Land Register as owner, without exclusion of indemnity (assuming that he was satisfied that there had been the necessary possession for 10 years).
(b) The same facts, but the disposition by Jack to Jill happens in 2006, not in 2003. The Keeper will either reject Jill's application altogether, or accept it with an exclusion of indemnity.
(c) Tina's title is based on an *a non domino* Tina-to-Tina disposition recorded in the Sasine Register in 1992. In 1997 Tina dispones to Lara, the disposition being recorded in the Sasine Register. In 2006 Lara dispones to Barbara, who applies for registration in the Land Register. The Keeper will either reject the application or will accept it with exclusion of indemnity. Assuming that Tina and Lara and Barbara have all possessed the property, when will the exclusion of indemnity be removed? The answer is 2007. This is on the assumption, which is probably correct and which is the Keeper's working assumption, that prescription on the Land Register can be aggregated with prescription on the Sasine Register.[1]

Suppose that Iona's title currently rests on an Iona-to-Iona disposition in the Sasine Register. If the *Aberdeen College* case is rightly decided, the prescriptive clock is not ticking. What should now be done? There is more than one possibility, but perhaps the simplest is to have a third party grant a new disposition in favour of Iona. This will be gratuitous, and so will enter the Sasine Register – if the Keeper will accept it. If he does, then at least the prescriptive clock will start to tick now.[2]

Finally, the *Aberdeen College* case may have implications for the way in which special destinations can be removed from a title. Because 2005 saw another important development in this area, we consider this issue separately.[3]

J A Pye (Oxford) Ltd v United Kingdom

The case itself

The *Pye* case[4] is one of the most important decisions that the European Court of Human Rights has ever made in the field of private law. The ultimate implications are unforeseeable. The fact that the technical quality of the decision is poor is little consolation.

---

1 For a discussion, see Scottish Law Commission, Discussion Paper on *Land Registration: Void and Voidable Titles* (Scot Law Com DP No 125, 2004; available on www.scotlawcom.gov.uk) para 3.10.
2 Of course, all these examples assume that prescription survives the decision in *Pye v United Kingdom*, as to which see below.
3 See p 74.
4 *J A Pye (Oxford) Ltd v United Kingdom*, 11 November 2005, European Court of Human Rights.

First, the story. J A Pye (Oxford) Ltd was a company that traded in land. Like many such companies, it bought rural land in the hope that planning permission would eventually be granted. One such plot of land was an area of about 50 acres in Berkshire. For a while it let neighbouring proprietors, the Grahams, use it for grazing, and a grazing rent was paid. But there came a time when the company thought that the existence of a grazing tenancy might be reducing its chances of getting planning permission. So the tenancy came to an end. Despite that, the Grahams simply carried on grazing their beasts on the land, without paying rent. This went on for 12 years, after which time the Grahams claimed that they were now the owners of the land. English law at that time had 12 years as the period of limitation (the equivalent of positive prescription), and without a requirement to have anything recorded or registered.

The Grahams won in the High Court,[1] but the judge said that the company's human rights had been violated, in the shape of Protocol 1 article 1 of the European Convention on Human Rights, which protects property rights. The company appealed, and the Court of Appeal reversed the decision on the ground that the nature of the Grahams' possession was insufficient to support a title by limitation.[2] Whereas the first instance judge felt that the law was with the Grahams but justice was with the company, the Court of Appeal felt that the law was with the company but justice was with the Grahams, or at least would have been had their possession been of the right quality. The Court of Appeal, unlike the court of first instance, did not consider that the company's human rights had been violated. The company now appealed to the House of Lords. The House of Lords reversed the decision of the Court of Appeal.[3] Its position was the same as that of the trial judge. On the basis of the legislation in force, the Grahams won, but the result, said the House of Lords, violated the company's human rights. But since the expiry of the 12-year period had happened before the Human Rights Act 1998 came into force, there was nothing that could be done as far as English law was concerned. So the company had lost. Since costs are seldom reported, it may be of interest to note that the company's own costs were £383,479.03. In addition it was ordered to pay the Grahams £424,000 in respect of their costs. Thus the company ended up paying over £800,000 in order to find out that it was no longer the owner of this plot of land.

But the company was persistent. Taking heed of the *obiter dicta* that its loss of the property might be contrary to the ECHR, the company sued the UK Government in the European Court of Human Rights.[4] The right to go to the Strasbourg Court dates from 1966 and does not depend on the Human Rights Act. Before we look at the Court's decision it is necessary to look a little more closely at English law.

---

1 *J A Pye (Oxford) Ltd v Graham* [2000] Ch 676.
2 *J A Pye (Oxford) Ltd v Graham* [2001] Ch 804.
3 *J A Pye (Oxford) Ltd v Graham* [2003] 1 AC 419, [2002] 3 All ER 865. For a study of the possession issue, see Oliver Radley-Gardner, 'Civilized squatting' (2005) 25 *Oxford Journal of Legal Studies* 727.
4 The company's costs in this action were £191,408.84. We do not know what the UK Government's costs were.

In Scotland, land that enters the Land Register was previously registered in the Sasine Register. But in England land that passes into the Land Registry was truly unregistered land.[1] Title to unregistered land depends on the deeds and on possession, and for such land limitation operated simply by 12 years of possession. Essentially the same rule was adopted for registered land. After 12 years of possession, actual title did not pass, but beneficial ownership passed, so that the registered owner held on constructive trust for the possessor. Thus in neither registered nor unregistered land was the running of limitation dependent on the registration of anything. In recent years rapid progress has been made in land registration, and the amount of unregistered land that is left is small and dwindling. In the *Pye* case the land was registered.

The Law Commission for England and Wales criticised the system in so far as it applied to registered land, noting that many other legal systems which had registration of title had severely restricted the scope of positive prescription.[2] It recommended that, for registered land, limitation should be allowed only in certain special cases. In particular, the registered owner had to be notified before title was lost. These recommendations were implemented by the Land Registration Act 2002,[3] but not retrospectively. The Commission's comments were to have an influence, not only on the 2002 Act, but also on the English courts and on the European Court of Human Rights. In *Pye* the English courts, encouraged by the Commission's views, said that the pre-2002 limitation regime did indeed violate the Convention.

In Strasbourg the company sued the UK Government for the value of the land, which it estimated at £10,000,000, plus all the costs it had incurred in the litigation in the English courts, plus all the costs it had been required to pay to the Grahams, plus its costs at Strasbourg. The Court split 4:3, the majority favouring the company.[4] As to damages the Court reserved judgment pending negotiations between the parties. It is understood that the UK Government is seeking leave to have the case reheard by the Grand Chamber. The decision and its implications are discussed below, but first it is necessary to bring in another important decision from 2005 on the same subject, *Beaulane Properties Ltd v Palmer*.[5]

Beaulane Properties Ltd v Palmer

This case was being litigated at the same time as *Pye*, and the two cases influenced each other. *Beaulane* was influenced by what the House of Lords said in *Pye*, while *Pye* (when at Strasbourg) was influenced by what was said in *Beaulane*. Though

---

1 There is a qualification: in two counties, Middlesex and Yorkshire, there was a register which worked rather like our Sasine Register.
2 Law Commission and HM Land Registry, *Land Registration for the Twenty-first Century: A Conveyancing Revolution* (Law Com No 271, 2001) paras 14.1–14.4.
3 Whilst making limitation far more difficult, the 2002 Act also reduced the period from 12 years to 10, which is of course the Scottish period.
4 The majority were M Pellonpää, V Strážnická, S Pavlovschi and the UK judge, N Bratza. The idiomatic style of the opinion perhaps suggests the authorship of the last. The minority judges were R Maruste, L Garlicki and J Borrego-Borrego.
5 [2005] 3 WLR 554.

only a first-instance decision, *Beaulane* may have significant implications. The basic facts in *Beaulane* were very similar to those in *Pye*. A company was the registered owner of green belt land.[1] A local man, Palmer, used it for grazing his beasts, paying no rent. After 12 years had passed, Palmer claimed a title by limitation. Thus far, thus like *Pye*. But there was one crucial difference. In *Pye* the 12-year period of adverse possession had been completed before the Human Rights Act 1998 came into force. There was thus in *Pye* no possibility of arguing that the Human Rights Act should trump the legislation on prescription, for the Grahams already had a good title: to apply the Human Rights Act would itself have been to violate the selfsame Act, for it would have been to deprive the Grahams of their property. But in *Beaulane* it was otherwise. The Human Rights Act had come into force shortly before the 12-year period had elapsed. The court took the view, in the first place, that the pre-2002 legislation on limitation was incompatible with Protocol 1 article 1 of the Convention, and, in the second place, that the legislation should be read so as to make it conform to (what the judge thought are) the requirements of the ECHR.

Pye and Beaulane: discussion

Are these decisions convincing? *Pye* was decided in the European Court of Human Rights by the narrowest of majorities, 4:3. The minority is scathing about the majority opinion, and one can understand why. Take para 50, where the majority writes:

> The Government argue that the position is different where, as in the present case, the relevant law exists at the time the property is acquired and where the operation of the law is to be seen as an incident of the property right at the time of its acquisition. The Court cannot accept the Government's argument. As registered freeholders, the applicants' title to the land was absolute and not subject to any restriction, qualification or limitation.

One rubs one's eyes. A circular argument is called by logicians a *petitio principii*. We have here a specimen. The UK Government points out that the company acquired a right which was, by law, defeasible in certain circumstances. The Court replies: the right was 'absolute and not subject to any restriction, qualification or limitation'. From that the court deduces (correctly, if trivially) that it was absolute and not subject to any restriction, qualification or limitation. But the premise was wrong, as counsel for the UK Government had carefully pointed out.[2]

The majority opinion attempts to justify its position thus:[3]

---

1 We do not know the county. The judgment merely says 'near Heathrow Airport': a chilling illustration of the loss of sense of place.
2 There are a number of types of situation in which ownership is defeasible. Sections 24 and 25 of the Sale of Goods Act 1979, which protect good faith purchasers, are examples. Must the UK Government now pay compensation to those divested by those provisions? We would suggest that the answer is negative. But the reason that it is negative is nothing to do with whether ownership is or is not 'absolute'.
3 Majority opinion para 51.

Article 1 does not cease to be engaged merely because a person acquires property subject to the provisions of the general law, the effect of which is in certain specified events to bring the property right to an end, and because those events have in fact occurred. Whether it does so will depend on whether the law in question is properly to be seen as qualifying or limiting the property right at the moment of acquisition or, whether it is rather to be seen as depriving the owner of an existing right at the point when the events occur and the law takes effect. It is only in the former case that Article 1 may be held to have no application.

The distinction being made here is far from clear.
A little later the majority opinion advances a different argument:

The Court … observes that, but for the provisions of the 1925 and 1980 Acts, the adverse possession of the land by the Grahams would have had no effect on the applicants' title or on their ability to repossess the land at any stage. It was the legislative provisions alone which deprived the applicants of their title and transferred the beneficial ownership to the Grahams and which thereby engaged the responsibility of the State under Article 1 of the Protocol.

Of course it is true that the legislation gave the property to the Grahams; but equally it had previously given the property to the company.
The majority opinion continues:[1]

The Government argue that the State has no duty to protect a person against his own negligence or inadvertence. The Court would, however, observe that such inadvertence would have had no adverse consequences for the applicants but for the contested statutory provisions.

One might point out that negligence would *never* have 'any adverse consequences' for *anyone* except for the fact that *the law so provides*. But when the Strasbourg Court does not like a legal provision it is classified as a mere 'contested statutory provision'. On this principle, anyone against whom delictual damages are awarded will be able to recover them from the UK Government because their human rights have been violated. We do not suggest that the Court would *actually* draw that conclusion. But the fact that they would *not* draw it shows the incoherence of the reasoning. The Court justifies the result in *Pye* by an appeal to a principle that cannot be seriously meant: like so much in so much of the ECHR case law, it is little more than a rhetorical device.

As the minority opinion notes, 'the real "fault" in this case, if there has been any, lies with the applicant companies, rather than the Government'.[2] It goes on to observe:

If the Government are responsible for the deprivation, what is the measure of their responsibility? In any event the loss of the land was not a deprivation of possessions or a confiscatory measure for which the payment of compensation would be appropriate.

---

1 Majority opinion para 74.
2 Minority opinion para 2. A Scots lawyer would be inclined to add that *vigilantibus non dormientibus jura subveniunt*, or, as Scott Wortley wittily translates it for his students, 'if you snooze, you lose'.

A finding that the companies were not responsible at all for the loss of their land – and that they should be compensated to the full value of the land at the taxpayer's expense – would run contrary to most people's notions of basic justice.[1]

Possible effect in Scotland

Unless the case is reheard with a different result, *Pye* could mean a large bill for UK taxpayers. It can be read as meaning that everyone who has lost title as a result of limitation or positive prescription has a potential claim for the value of the lost property.

One of the many worrying features of *Pye* is that the court says so little. It says only that limitation (or prescription), without compensation, is unlawful where the ousted owner has a title in a land register of the English type. What would have been held if the land had been unregistered? What if it had been registered in our Sasine Register? What if it had been registered in our Land Register? What if it had been registered in the German *Grundbuch*?[2] Across Europe national governments are, no doubt, looking at *Pye* and wondering whether or not their own laws are Strasbourg-proof. And few clear answers will emerge.

The High Court in *Beaulane*, and the House of Lords in *Pye*, indicated that prescription may be justified in a wholly unregistered system, but cannot be justified, at least without safeguards, in a system such as the English registration system. The Strasbourg court quotes such comments, for example Lord Bingham's statement that:[3]

> Where land is registered it is difficult to see any justification for a legal rule which compels such an apparently unjust result, and even harder to see why the party gaining title should not be required to pay some compensation at least to the party losing it.

But the Strasbourg court itself does not lay so much emphasis on the registered/unregistered distinction as on two other features of the pre-2002 English system, namely (i) lack of notice to the owner, and (ii) lack of compensation.

Our Land Register is on the whole similar to its English equivalent, which is not surprising since the Land Registration (Scotland) Act 1979 was to a substantial extent based on the English legislation. But there are many differences, great and small, and one such difference, as it happens, lies in the area of prescription and limitation. Under the pre-2002 English law (with which *Pye* and *Beaulane* were concerned), limitation required possession for 12 years but did *not* require anything equivalent to our foundation writ. By contrast, in Scots law prescription cannot start to run unless and until the person seeking to acquire title has recorded an appropriate deed or registered a title. This is obviously a significant difference from English law, but whether it means that our law is Strasbourg-proof is difficult to say.[4] Although not actual notice to the

---

1 Minority opinion para 4.
2 On which a number of other countries have also modelled their land registration systems.
3 Quoted at para 71.
4 For a brief first reaction, see Ken Swinton, 'Prescription, human rights and the Land Register: *Pye v UK*' (2005) 73 *Scottish Law Gazette* 179.

owner, registration makes it easier for the owner to find out that the prescriptive clock may be ticking against him.

One possible position is that positive prescription is still – post-*Pye* – permissible in the Sasine Register but not in the Land Register. But it is equally possible that it is permissible in both, or that it is permissible in neither. What the Scottish Executive will do remains to be seen.

In the light of *Pye* and *Beaulane*, the Keeper's decision, in the mid-1990s, to become much more cautious about accepting *a non domino* dispositions now seems a most fortunate one. And the Scottish Executive may regard the *Aberdeen College* decision with favour, for every case in which it is held that positive prescription has not taken place is one case fewer in which there is a potential damages claim against the state for having violated human rights. The *Beaulane* case tends in the same direction.

Of course, *Beaulane* is only a first-instance decision, and so its weight as a precedent is limited even in England, and doubly so in Scotland. Whether it would be followed here is impossible to say. One of the problems has already been mentioned: the Scottish rules about prescription are different. Another is that there may perhaps be doubt as to whether the court in *Beaulane* was right to treat the 1998 Act as virtually amending the conveyancing legislation. In a non-conveyancing case in 2005, *Robbie the Pict v Miller Buidheann Ltd*,[1] Sheriff Principal Bowen had this to say:

> In terms of s 3 of the Human Rights Act (headed 'Interpretation of Legislation') primary legislation must be read and given effect in a way which is compatible with Convention rights. It is expressly provided in sub-section (2)(b) that the section 'does not affect the validity, continuing operation or enforcement of any incompatible legislation'. What this means is that if there is ambiguity in the meaning of a statute the court must choose the interpretation which is compatible with Convention rights. If there is no such ambiguity the court must apply the statute even if the terms are not so compatible.[2]

We would respectfully agree with this succinct statement. But the fact is that many judges, particularly in England, have been taking a more radical approach, using the Human Rights Act as a tool to alter legislation to make it conform to justice as they see it.

Implications for other forms of prescription

Pye was a case about the acquisition of ownership. There are other forms of positive prescription too, such as the prescriptive acquisition of a servitude of way (which, be it noted, does not require any foundation writ). Negative prescription can also operate in property law, such as the loss of a servitude by non-use. Whether such prescription remains lawful in the light of *Pye* is, like so much else, unclear.

Indeed, the ramifications might go further. Up to now, attacks on the negative prescription of rights to debt or to damages, as being a violation of

---

1 9 November 2005, Portree Sheriff Court, A93/04.
2 Paragraph 24.

human rights, have failed, the leading case being *Stubbings v United Kingdom*.[1] But these attacks have been based on article 6 (right to a fair trial etc). In *Pye* the attack was based not on article 6 but on Protocol 1 article 1 (the property protection clause). If it is a violation of human rights to lose land worth, say, £10,000 after 10 years, is it any the less a violation of human rights to lose a right to be paid say £1,000,000 after just five years? A right to money can be lost by mere forgetfulness. A right of property can be lost only if someone else is in visible occupation for 10 years: so the law makes it much easier to lose a right to money than a right of property. In the light of *Pye*, negative prescription too may now be in question.

SPECIAL DESTINATIONS

Special destinations are in the news twice this year. The Family Law (Scotland) Act 2006 has provisions about revocation by divorce. And the decision in *Board of Management of Aberdeen College v Youngson*[2] has raised questions about consensual *inter vivos* revocation.

Family Law (Scotland) Act 2006

Section 19 provides:

(1) Subsections (2) and (3) apply where –
    (a) heritable property is held in the name of –
        (i) a person ('A') and A's spouse ('B') and the survivor of them;
        (ii) A, B and another person and the survivor or survivors of them;
        (iii) A with a special destination on A's death, in favour of B;
    (b) A and B's marriage is terminated by divorce or annulment; and
    (c) after the divorce or annulment A dies.
(2) In relation to the succession to A's heritable property (or part of it) under the destination, B shall be deemed to have failed to survive A.
(3) If a person has in good faith and for value (whether by purchase or otherwise) acquired title to the heritable property, the title so acquired shall not be challengeable on the ground that, by virtue of subsection (2), the property falls to the estate of A.
(4) Subsection (2) shall not apply if the destination specifies that B is to take under the destination despite the termination of A and B's marriage by divorce or annulment.

Schedule 1 makes the corresponding change for civil partners by inserting a new s 124A into the Civil Partnership Act 2004.

---

1 (1996) 23 EHRR 213.
2 [2005] CSOH 31, 2005 SC 335, 2005 SLT 371. Another aspect of this case was discussed at p 63 above.

The provision is technically well drafted, and one would guess that the underlying policy has fairly widespread support. Leaving the finer points on one side, the section says that if spouses divorce, and later one of them dies, the surviving ex-spouse cannot benefit from any special destination in the title to any heritable property[1] belonging to the deceased ex-spouse. As we read it, it applies only to future divorces, and so will have no effect in relation to divorces prior to the date when the section comes into force.

From a practical point of view, the section covers two main types of case. In the *first* type, Jack and Jill are married and buy a house together. There is a survivorship destination. Then they divorce.[2] Nothing is done about the title to the house, where Jill continues to live. Jack dies. Under current law Jill (assuming she is still alive[3]) will inherit Jack's half share. That is certainly the case if he dies intestate, and almost certainly the case if he dies testate. The latter depends on whether the destination was or was not evacuable. In most cases it will be found to be unevacuable, so that Jill's right trumps the right of a legatee.[4] Under the new law, the special destination ceases to have effect on divorce. When Jack dies, his share of the house is simply part of his estate.

The *second* type of case is the following. Adam and Eve are married. They buy a house together. There is a survivorship destination. They divorce. She dispones to him her half share in the house. Later he dies, still owning the house. His original half share now reverts to her (assuming she is still alive).[5]

Neither of these situations is particularly common. As for the first, upon a divorce (or upon the pre-divorce separation) it is likely that either (i) the property will be sold, or (ii) one of the parties will become sole owner. As for the second, the danger has become fairly well known, and for many years now conveyancers have generally drafted the disposition as a disposition of the whole property by Adam and Eve in favour of Adam: this is generally thought (see below) to 'wash out' the destination from the title. But such cases, though not common, do crop up. The legislation will not have retrospective effect, but will apply only to divorces which happen after the legislation comes into force.

Go back to the first case: Jack and Jill. Suppose that after Jack's death Jill offers the (whole) property for sale. The buyer will see that the title has a survivorship destination, and that Jack has died. The buyer pays the price. Then Jack's executor knocks at the door and points out that, under s 19, the effect of the divorce was to revoke the destination, so that Jill had the right to sell only her half share, not the whole property. The problem here is that the fact of the divorce will not

---

1 The section is limited to heritable property. Arguably it should have been extended to special destinations in (incorporeal) moveable property. But the point is not an important one, for such cases are uncommon.

2 In books of popular science we read that physical processes are in principle reversible, so that there is a problem about how to define 'time's arrow'. Physicists should perhaps be told that time's arrow could be defined through family law, for lovers marry first, divorce later.

3 If the beneficiary ('substitute' is the technical term) of a special destination dies, the benefit does not form part of his/her estate. A special destination is personal to the beneficiary.

4 See G L Gretton and K G C Reid, *Conveyancing* (3rd edn 2004) ch 23.

5 *Gardner's Exrs v Raeburn* 1996 SLT 745.

appear on the Land Register (or Sasine Register), so the buyer may not know about it. Nevertheless the buyer has a double protection. In the first place, as a proprietor in possession he is protected against rectification unless he has been careless (or fraudulent).[1] But in addition to that general rule, the new legislation expressly provides that the buyer will be protected by good faith.[2]

We shall have to see how practice handles this issue. When buying from someone who can point to (a) a survivorship destination, and (b) the death certificate of her spouse, it might be worth obtaining and preserving evidence of good faith by including an extra few words at the end of the affidavit (or its replacement, the written declaration)[3] which the seller will have to produce in any case.[4] A possible wording might be:

> I further declare[5] that my marriage to my late husband Dan Dare was terminated neither by divorce nor by annulment but by his death on [*date*].

Section 19(3) protects only a person who 'has in good faith and for value … acquired title'. Thus it does not protect someone who takes by gift or succession. What about, say, the grantee of a standard security, or of a lease? If 'title' means *any* real right then they would be protected. But 'title' is a word with a range of meanings, and possibly here it means ownership alone.

The new provision operates only upon divorce (and annulment). From that fact it is worth drawing out two consequences. The first is that the new provision can never benefit a couple who live together as if they were married, and who later part. To receive the benefits of divorce it is necessary first to get married. The second consequence is that the new provision does not benefit spouses who separate but who have not yet divorced. The period can be lengthy, and indeed some spouses who part never divorce. Of course separation may be exactly the moment when one party, or both, wishes to make a will leaving his or her share to someone else. Yet if that person dies before the divorce, the legacy is likely to be ineffective because most destinations are non-evacuable. At this point it is worth remembering that when a survivorship destination is created it is always competent to include a declaration of evacuability: 'But expressly declaring that the said grantees and each of them shall have full right and power to evacuate the foregoing destination.'

Washing out the destination: general principles

How is a special destination evacuated? Here is a chart showing the common law principles. (Section 19 of the Family Law (Scotland) Act 2006, discussed above, is an extra and is not included.)

---

1 Land Registration (Scotland) Act 1979 s 9(3)(a)(iii).
2 Family Law (Scotland) Act 2006 s 19.
3 Family Law (Scotland) Act 2006 s 6(3). See p 79.
4 Unless he or she has remarried.
5 This is a style for a written declaration: see p 80. For an affidavit 'declare' should be replaced by 'swear' or 'affirm'.

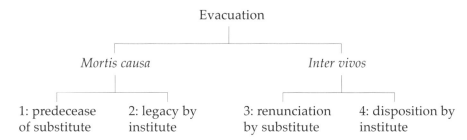

In a special destination, the 'institute' is the owner, and the 'substitute' is the person to whom (if still alive) the property will presumptively pass at the institute's death. Nowadays the only type of special destination commonly encountered is the survivorship destination. Here one half is conveyed to Jack as institute with Jill as substitute, and the other half is conveyed to Jill with Jack as substitute. In the chart there are four cases of evacuation. They divide into *mortis causa* evacuation (methods 1 and 2) and *inter vivos* evacuation (methods 3 and 4). But they also divide in another manner: by act of the substitute (methods 1 and 3) or by act of the institute (methods 2 and 4). Another way of setting it out would be:

	Mortis causa	*Inter vivos*
Substitutes's act	1: predecease	3: renunciation
Institute's act	2: legacy	4: disposition

In method 1, the substitute fails to survive the institute. For instance, Jack and Jill co-own property with a survivorship destination. Jack dies intestate. His share passes to Jill. She dies a week later. Her original half share does not now pass to Jack's estate, the reason being that in relation to this half share Jack was substitute, and he has not survived the institute.

In method 2 the institute dies, and bequeaths the share to a third party. For instance, Jack leaves his share to his brother, Bob. This may or may not evacuate the destination, depending on the circumstances. It will evacuate it (with the result that Bob inherits the share) if both (a) Jack had the power of *mortis causa* evacuation, and (b) he validly exercised that power. As for (b) the rules are contained in s 30 of the Succession (Scotland) Act 1964. As for (a), one first looks at the deed which constituted the destination to see if it contains any express statement as to whether the destination can be evacuated. Such statements are unusual but not unknown.[1] If the deed is silent, one applies the presumptions established by the case law, as a result of which the destination will usually be found to be unevacuable.[2] However, if both parties are prepared

---

1 In our view it is good practice to state expressly that the destination is or is not capable of evacuation by legacy.

2 See in particular *Perrett's Trs v Perrett* 1909 SC 522. For a review of the case law see M Morton, 'Special destinations as testamentary instructions' 1984 SLT (News) 133.

to co-operate, this bar to evacuation can be waived. Thus Jack and Jill could each authorise the other to evacuate by method 2. It should be stressed that this waiver falls short of a complete renunciation (method 3), because it does not revoke the destination with immediate effect. Thus if Jack has the power to evacuate by method 2 but in fact dies intestate, the destination will apply to his share of the property, and not the rules of intestate succession. And even if he does die testate, the destination will still take effect if he fails to word the legacy in conformity with the requirements of s 30 of the 1964 Act.

In method 3 the substitute renounces the destination with immediate effect. This kills the destination at once, so that even if the institute were to die intestate the destination would not take effect.[1] Renunciations are generally done by a deed that is not registered in either the Sasine or Land Register. And here a small point of uncertainty exists. Suppose Jack renounces the benefit of the destination. Jill then dies. Clearly Jill's share passes to her estate, even if she has died intestate. That is not in doubt. The doubt is not one of substantive right, but as to conveyancing. On one view, the destination still operates so as to transfer to Jack the title to Jill's half share, this happening because of the doctrine of so-called automatic infeftment. The result would then be that Jack would have been unjustifiably enriched and would therefore be bound immediately to dispone the half share back to Jill's executors. The other view is that the unregistered renunciation takes effect not only as to substantive right but also as to title, so that Jill's share would never pass to Jack, even temporarily. Which of these two views is correct is uncertain. Although the second seems right in principle, it fails to observe the publicity principle by giving effect as respects title to an off-register deed.[2]

In method 4, the institute transfers ownership to someone else. In the case of a survivorship destination, what is transferred is a *pro indiviso* share. The reason this operates as evacuation is that a special destination cannot take effect unless the institute still owns the property at the time of death. Thus Jack could dispone his share to his brother. Or he could dispone it to Jill. That will evacuate the destination attached to his share, but in and of itself the disposition would not affect the destination attached to Jill's original half share.[3]

Washing out the destination: which powder washes whiter?

Under the Family Law (Scotland) Act 2006 s 19, divorce revokes special desti-nations. But parties will often wish to evacuate without (or at least in advance

---

1 We are not aware of direct express authority, but the competency of renunciation is clear in principle. This was also the *ius commune* rule: see Voet, *Commentarius ad Pandectas* 36.1.65, dealing with fideicommissary substitution (*substitutio fideicommaria*) of which our special destination is a type. Of course, there are the usual qualifications about parties who have become incapax, been sequestrated etc.

2 The ultimate source of the problem is the doctrine of automatic infeftment itself. The doctrine was introduced by *Bisset v Walker* 26 Nov 1799 FC, a wrongly-decided case that continues to do its mischief.

3 *Gardner's Exrs v Raeburn* 1996 SLT 745.

of) divorce. There are typically two types of case. (a) Brad and Jennifer co-own a house with a survivorship destination. They are separating, and it has been agreed that Jennifer is to have the house. They wish to make sure that if Jennifer dies before Brad, and still owns the house at the time of her death, Brad will not inherit Jennifer's original half share.[1] (b) Fred and Ginger co-own a house with a survivorship destination. They are not separating, and neither is transferring his/her share to the other. Nevertheless, each wants that share to form part of his or her own estate in the event of death, and not necessarily to pass to the survivor.

One approach is to use method 2 above (legacy by institute). If the destination contains a bar to evacuation, there can always be a deed in which this is waived. Provided the legacy is worded to conform to the requirements of s 30 of the Succession (Scotland) Act 1964, method 2 will work. But it is in some ways rather unattractive. It does not kill off the destination immediately, but depends on the making of a valid s 30 legacy.

Sometimes method 3 is used: renunciation. While in principle this is effective, the practice has not been to attempt to register the renunciation in the Land or Sasine Register. This is inconvenient in that the fact of the renunciation can later be overlooked. There is also the doubt mentioned above as to whether this method will exclude the possibility of 'automatic infeftment'.

Method 4 happens whenever the property is being sold. But it is also commonly relied on in other cases. In case (a) above, Brad and Jennifer dispone to Jennifer but without the destination. The general belief is that this will remove the original destination so that, for example, if Jennifer dies the next week, her original half share will not pass to Jack. In case (b), Fred and Ginger dispone to themselves, omitting the destination, and here too the general belief is that this will remove the destination completely. However, as a result of the decision in *Board of Management of Aberdeen College v Youngson*,[2] there has been concern about whether method 4 really works in such cases. In case (b), the Fred and Ginger case, the same parties are granters and grantees – as the Youngsons were in *Aberdeen College*. In case (a), where Brad and Jennifer dispone to Jennifer, Jennifer is, to the extent of a half share, disponing to herself. And it is that half share that is the main concern, for the worry would be that if Jennifer dies, her original share might be subject to an unevacuated destination. In short, in both cases the dispositions are not dispositions wholly in favour of third parties, and so their effectiveness might perhaps be questioned in the light of the *Aberdeen College* decision. For instance, the Lord Ordinary says that 'a deed or conveyance whereby a person purports to sell to himself does not involve any transfer nor any delivery. Without some independent third party or separate persona, it is no transaction at all.'[3]

In our view there is no cause for concern, and dispositions of types (a) and (b) are effective to evacuate the destination from the title.[4] It is true that in case

---

1 This is the problem of *Gardner's Exrs v Raeburn* 1996 SLT 745, mentioned above.
2 [2005] CSOH 31, 2005 SC 335, 2005 SLT 371. *Kenneil v Kenneil* [2006] CSOH 8 should also be noted. This case will be discussed in next year's volume.
3 Paragraph 2.
4 While the Keeper has not made any formal pronouncement, our understanding is that he takes the same view.

(b) no right of ownership is being transferred, because the grantees are already the owners. But the parties are altering the terms of the infeftment.[1] As is pointed out in *Professor McDonald's Conveyancing Manual*,[2] under the older law an owner was free to dispone to himself for the purpose of creating a new destination. For instance, X could dispone to himself, with a special destination to, say, his heirs male. The validity of such a disposition was beyond question, even though it did not actually transfer ownership.

Nevertheless, to help settle nerves jangled by the *Aberdeen College* decision, we would suggest that a clause of renunciation be added to the disposition – whether the Fred and Ginger type or the Brad and Jennifer type. Method 4 would thus be fortified by method 3, so that if the disposition were deemed inept, the renunciation would be valid on its own. The clause could be conveniently inserted at or near the end of the deed. A possible clause is the following:

> And considering that hitherto we have held the said subjects as *pro indiviso* heritable proprietors under the special destination aftermentioned, and further considering that our intention is that the said special destination be wholly renounced, revoked and evacuated, as if it had never been constituted, therefore we each of us, with mutual consent, do hereby renounce revoke and evacuate, as from the date of these presents, the survivorship destination contained in [*specify deed and details of registration*]....

Under current practice, the disposition of type (b) (the Fred and Ginger case) often contains a narrative clause about the intention to evacuate. That is good, but narrative is not quite the same as a *de praesenti* declaration, and so we would still suggest the use of the words of renunciation. As for dispositions of type (a) (the Brad and Jennifer case), it is not usual for the narrative to say anything about evacuation, so the addition of words of *de praesenti* renunciation is even more desirable. But all this is simply an insurance policy: it seems to us that the traditional practice is effective anyway.

OCCUPANCY RIGHTS

Introduction

To the occupancy rights of non-entitled spouses under the Matrimonial Homes (Family Protection) (Scotland) Act 1981 have now been added, with effect from 5 December 2005, the occupancy rights of civil partners[3] under the Civil Partnership Act 2004.[4] Although contained in different Acts, the legislative provisions are virtually identical. The Family Law (Scotland) Act 2006 will,

---

1 To use traditional terminology. Strictly speaking, since the abolition of feudal tenure the term 'infeftment' should not be used.
2 7th edn 2004, by David Brand, Andrew Steven and Scott Wortley, at para 12.7. The argument is as sound as it is ingenious.
3 Ie same-sex couples who have entered into a civil partnership under the Civil Partnership Act 2004.
4 Civil Partnership Act 2004 (Commencement No 2) (Scotland) Order 2005, SSI 2005/604.

when in force, amend both sets of provisions. The amendments derive from a Report of the Scottish Law Commission published as long ago as 1992.[1]

Affidavits/written declarations

Since 5 December 2005 it has been necessary to ensure that affidavits, where they are needed (typically where the granter is unmarried), cover civil partners as well as spouses. That could be done by using two separate affidavits but a combined affidavit is obviously more convenient. A style for a combined affidavit (whether on sale or on the granting of a security) would be:

I, AB [*design*], do solemnly and sincerely swear [*or* affirm] that as at this date the property known as [*address*] is not

(i) a matrimonial home in relation to which a spouse of mine has occupancy rights within the meaning of the Matrimonial Homes (Family Protection) (Scotland) Act 1981, or

(ii) a family home in relation to which a civil partner of mine has occupancy rights within the meaning of the Civil Partnership Act 2004.

'Family home' is the equivalent of 'matrimonial home' in respect of civil partners.

Once it is in force, the Family Law (Scotland) Act 2006 will replace affidavits with a simple written declaration signed by the granter.[2] A witness, though not needed, would give the benefit of probativity. The reason for the change is said to be the difficulty of finding notaries public in rural areas.[3] A false declaration is an offence under the False Oaths (Scotland) Act 1933,[4] and the Scottish Law Commission suggests that forms sent out for signature by solicitors should contain a prominent statement warning that a false declaration could be an offence.[5] Notaries will continue to be needed for renunciations, which are unaffected by the reform.

Affidavits are separate documents, and declarations could be done in the same way. But now that notaries are no longer needed, the declaration could simply be included as a clause of the disposition. It makes practical sense to have one signed document instead of two, and incorporation in the disposition eliminates the danger of accidental loss. The declaration could be placed at or near the end of the deed.

Presumably due to oversight, affidavits are replaced only in the case of sales (now recast more broadly as transfers for value)[6] and not in respect of the

---

1 Scottish Law Commission, Report on *Family Law* (Scot Law Com No 135, 1992) part XI.
2 Family Law (Scotland) Act 2006 s 6(3).
3 Scottish Law Commission, Report on *Family Law* paras 11.16 and 11.17.
4 False Oaths (Scotland) Act 1933 s 2. The maximum penalty is two years' imprisonment.
5 Scottish Law Commission, Report on *Family Law* para 11.17.
6 Ie Matrimonial Homes (Family Protection) (Scotland) Act 1981 s 6(3)(e); Civil Partnership Act 2004 s 106(3)(e).

grant of standard securities.[1] So where a standard security is being granted, an affidavit should continue to be used in the form given above, but for sales and other transfers for value (eg excambions) the affidavit is replaced by a written declaration. However, it is possible that the 2006 Act will be amended, perhaps even before it comes into force, to extend written declarations to standard securities.[2]

The relevant provisions for written declarations are s 6(3)(e) of the Matrimonial Homes (Family Protection) (Scotland) Act 1981 and s 106(3)(e) of the Civil Partnership Act, as amended by the Family Law Act. Following the amendment, s 6(3)(e) of the 1981 Act will read:[3]

> This section shall not apply in any case where –
>
> …
>
> (e) the dealing comprises a transfer for value to a third party who has acted in good faith if there is produced to the third party by the transferor –
>
> (i) a written declaration signed by the transferor, or a person acting on behalf of the transferor under a power of attorney or as a guardian (within the meaning of the Adults with Incapacity (Scotland) Act 2000 (asp 4)), that the subjects of the transfer are not, or were not at the time of the dealing, a matrimonial home in relation to which a spouse of the transferor has or had occupancy rights; or
>
> (ii) a renunciation of occupancy rights or consent to the dealing which bears to have been properly made or given by the non-entitled spouse or a person acting on behalf of the non-entitled spouse under a power of attorney or as a guardian (within the meaning of the Adults with Incapacity (Scotland) Act 2000 (asp 4)).

Apart from the difference in execution, the form of a written declaration will be almost identical to that of an affidavit. If a separate document is used, a declaration might read as follows:

> I, AB [design], hereby declare that as at this date the property known as [address] is not
>
> (i) a matrimonial home in relation to which a spouse of mine has occupancy rights within the meaning of the Matrimonial Homes (Family Protection) (Scotland) Act 1981, or
>
> (ii) a family home in relation to which a civil partner of mine has occupancy rights within the meaning of the Civil Partnership Act 2004.

---

1 Ie Matrimonial Homes (Family Protection) (Scotland) Act 1981 s 8(2A); Civil Partnership Act 2004 s 108(3).

2 Section 44 of the Act confers power to make consequential amendments by statutory instrument.

3 Family Law (Scotland) Act 2006 s 6(3). The equivalent change to s 106(3)(e) of the Civil Partnership Act 2004 is made by sch 1 para 4(b) of the 2006 Act. An omission from the new version is the sentence: 'For the purposes of this paragraph, the time of the dealing, in the case of the sale of an interest in heritable property, is the date of delivery to the purchaser of the deed transferring title to that interest.'

Where the declaration is included as a clause in the disposition, the opening words would become 'and I hereby declare that …'.

What if, after the 2006 Act comes into force, an affidavit is used instead of a written declaration? On the principle that the greater includes the lesser, such an affidavit would in our view be valid. Section 6(3)(e) of the 1981 Act, as amended, requires merely 'a written declaration signed by the transferor'. An affidavit is signed, and to swear or affirm a state of facts is also, presumably, to declare them. So while a written declaration could not be an affidavit, it may be taken that an affidavit can be a written declaration.

Guardians and attorneys

Can the guardian of an incapable adult grant documentation in respect of occupancy rights? Can an agent acting under a power of attorney do so? The view generally held is that guardians and attorneys can grant renunciations and consents but not affidavits.[1] The position is changed by the 2006 Act so that guardians and attorneys will also be able to grant written declarations (the replacement for affidavits).[2] The provision presupposes[3] that a dealing by a guardian is a dealing by the adult, for if it was not there would be no need for documentation. As it is, the document required is a written declaration/affidavit from the guardian, or a consent or renunciation from the adult's spouse or civil partner.

Reluctant spouse/civil partner

Occasionally a non-entitled spouse or civil partner refuses to consent to a dealing. In that situation two provisions in the Family Law (Scotland) Act 2006 come to the assistance of the entitled spouse.

The first applies only where the parties have lived apart for two years, and the non-entitled spouse or civil partner has not been occupying the property home. On the basis that, under the Act, either party would be entitled to divorce,[4] it is provided that occupancy rights are extinguished by two years' non-cohabitation and non-occupancy.[5] Following such extinction, the entitled spouse or civil partner would then be in a position to make a declaration or affidavit as to the absence of occupancy rights.

---

1 See eg G L Gretton and K G C Reid, *Conveyancing* (3rd edn 2004) para 10-16.
2 Matrimonial Homes (Family Protection) (Scotland) Act 1981 s 6(3)(e), amended by the Family Law (Scotland) Act 2006 s 6(3); Civil Partnership Act 2004 s 106(3)(e), amended by the Family Law (Scotland) Act 2006 sch 1 para 4(b). Direct provision is confined to written declarations, but the reference in the amendments to renunciations and consents – the substantive provision for which occurs elsewhere in the legislation and is unamended – supposes that it is already the law that these can be granted by guardians and attorneys.
3 Contrary to the view held by the Keeper: see *Conveyancing 2002* pp 106–107.
4 Divorce (Scotland) Act 1976 s 1(2)(e), amended by the Family Law (Scotland) Act 2006 s 11(b).
5 Matrimonial Homes (Family Protection) (Scotland) Act 1981 s 1(7), inserted by the Family Law (Scotland) Act 2006 s 4; Civil Partnership Act 2004 s 101(6A), inserted by the Family Law (Scotland) Act 2006 sch 1 para 2.

The second relates to the existing mechanism for applying to the court to dispense with consent.[1] In *Fyfe v Fyfe*[2] it was held, logically if inconveniently, that the court could not dispense with consent unless it was reasonably clear what the proposed dealing would entail, including, in the case of a sale, the price. So no blanket dispensation could be given for sale before a house was put on the market. The position is changed by the Family Law Act, making it possible to obtain a dispensation for a future sale, subject to the court fixing a minimum price, and a deadline for concluding the contract.[3]

Where an application for a dispensing order is refused, the court can order the non-entitled spouse or civil partner to pay rent to the owner (whether the entitled spouse/partner or, following a dealing, a third party), and to comply with such other conditions in relation to occupation as the court may specify.[4]

Defective documentation: current transaction

Even if the documentation – affidavit/declaration, renunciation, or consent – in the current transaction turns out to be defective, the grantee, if in good faith, is usually protected.[5] That is already the law and it is not changed by the Family Law (Scotland) Act 2006. But if there is no documentation, or if the documentation is defective to the eye, or if the transaction was neither a sale nor a security with the result that the statutory protection does not apply, the grantee is vulnerable to the assertion of an occupancy right until prescription has run.[6] The Family Law Act reduces the period of prescription from five years to two while providing, contrary to the decision in *Stevenson v Roy*,[7] that no account is taken of any time during which the spouse or civil partner was attempting to assert the occupancy rights in court.[8] As before, prescription requires both that the *entitled* spouse or partner has permanently ceased to be entitled to occupy the home (which is likely to be the effect of the current transaction) and also that the *non-entitled* spouse or partner has not been in occupation for the prescriptive period.

---

1 Matrimonial Homes (Family Protection) Scotland) Act 1981 s 7; Civil Partnership Act 2004 s 107.
2 1987 SLT (Sh Ct) 38.
3 Matrimonial Homes (Family Protection) (Scotland) Act 1981 s 7(1A), (1B), inserted by the Family Law (Scotland) Act 2006 s 7(b); Civil Partnership Act 2004 s 107(1A), (1B), inserted by the Family Law (Scotland) Act 2006 sch 1 para 5(b).
4 Matrimonial Homes (Family Protection) (Scotland) Act 1981 s 7(3A), inserted by the Family Law (Scotland) Act 2006 s 7(c); Civil Partnership Act 2004 s 107(3A), inserted by the Family Law (Scotland) Act 2006 sch 1 para 5(c).
5 Matrimonial Homes (Family Protection) (Scotland) Act 1981 ss 6(3)(e), 8; Civil Partnership Act 2004 ss 106(3)(e), 108.
6 Matrimonial Homes (Family Protection) (Scotland) Act 1981 s 6(3)(f); Civil Partnership Act 2004 s 106(3)(f).
7 2003 SC 544, noted in *Conveyancing 2003* p 24.
8 Family Law (Scotland) Act 2006 ss 6(3)(b), 8 and sch 1 paras 4(b)(iii), 6. These insert a new s 9A into the Matrimonial Homes Act and a new s 111A into the Civil Partnership Act.

Defective documentation: previous transactions

Almost always, a house which is already on the Land Register will have, on its title sheet, a statement by the Keeper that there are no subsisting occupancy rights of spouses or civil partners of former owners.[1] That makes further enquiry unnecessary, for, even if the statement is wrong, it is covered by the Keeper's indemnity. So a person buying a house which is on the Register is concerned only with occupancy rights connected with the current owner.

For Sasine titles (including first registrations) the position is different. Except where they are seeking to rely on prescription (which, as just seen, requires evidence of non-possession), purchasers must check the documentation for previous transactions. Indeed in theory this should be done right back to the coming into force of the Matrimonial Homes (Family Protection) (Scotland) Act 1981, on 1 September 1982. Admittedly, there is an argument that occupancy rights do not survive a second transfer, for the relevant section provides that occupancy rights are not prejudiced 'by reason *only*' of any dealing of the entitled spouse or partner,[2] and a further sale by the person who first bought from the entitled spouse or partner might be thought to take matters beyond the 'only'. But the position is unclear, and in practice it is assumed that occupancy rights do survive.

The position is changed by the Family Law (Scotland) Act 2006, which inserts a new s 6(1A) into the 1981 Act.[3] It reads:

> The occupancy rights of a non-entitled spouse in relation to a matrimonial home shall not be exercisable in relation to the home where, following a dealing of the entitled spouse relating to the home –
>
> (a) a person acquires the home, or an interest in it, in good faith and for value from a person other than the person who is or, as the case may be, was the entitled spouse; or
>
> (b) a person derives title to the home from a person who acquired title as mentioned in paragraph (a).

An equivalent provision is added to the Civil Partnership Act.[4]

It is not certain when a home is 'acquired' for the purposes of this provision, but probably a home is acquired only when the title of the acquirer has been completed by registration. Nor is it certain what is mean by 'an interest' in the home, but it probably covers fractional rights of ownership rather than other types of real right such as standard security.[5] Indeed if standard securities were to be included, occupancy rights would be defeated every time the first acquirer funded the purchase by a loan.

---

1 Land Registration (Scotland) Rules 1980, SI 1980/1413, r 5(j) (spouses). For civil partners the statement is non-statutory: see Registers of Scotland, *Update 19*, available on www.ros.gov.uk/updates.

2 Matrimonial Homes (Family Protection) (Scotland) Act 1981 s 6(1); Civil Partnership Act 2004 s 106(1).

3 Family Law (Scotland) Act 2006 s 6(2).

4 Civil Partnership Act 2004 s 106(1A), inserted by the Family Law (Scotland) Act 2006 sch 1 para 4(a).

5 Scottish Law Commission, Report on *Family Law* (Scot Law Com No 135, 1992) paras 11.10–11.12.

It is assumed that there is no duty of enquiry, so that acquirers are in good faith so long as they do not know, as positive fact, that the home was burdened by the occupancy right of the spouse or partner of a previous owner. Indeed any other view would defeat the purpose of the provision. The result is a welcome simplification of conveyancing. In a Sasine transaction or first registration it will no longer be necessary to consider the position of former owners: documentation is required only in respect of the current owner.

SERVITUDES

It is often said that servitudes can be constituted

- expressly, by writing followed by registration[1]
- by implication in a break-off conveyance
- by positive prescription
- by acquiescence.[2]

Three of these methods of creation were the subject of important decisions in 2005 (the exception was prescription),[3] and indeed doubt was expressed as to whether a servitude could be created by acquiescence at all.[4] In addition, as in the last two years, there was a significant development in the law as it relates to servitudes of parking.

Creation: express servitudes

What deeds?

Can a servitude be created in a deed of conditions? Or, to express the question more precisely, can a servitude be created in a deed of conditions *alone* without also being incorporated into a subsequent conveyance? We imagine that most conveyancers would give as an answer an unhesitating 'yes'. But in *Candleberry Ltd v West End Homeowners Association*[5] the answer was said to be 'no'.

In *Candleberry* a deed of conditions recorded in 1989 provided that:

> Each proprietor shall have a heritable and irredeemable right of access for vehicular and pedestrian access over the 'public areas' which are shaded in yellow and pale green on the aforesaid plan.

---

1 For the registration requirement see the Title Conditions (Scotland) Act 2003 s 75.
2 For other possible methods of creation, see D J Cusine and R R M Paisley, *Servitudes and Rights of Way* (1998) ch 11.
3 Although of course the decision in *J A Pye (Oxford) Ltd v United Kingdom* 15 November 2005, European Court of Human Rights, may have implications for the future of servitudes by prescription. See pp 65–72 above.
4 *Moncrieff v Jamieson* 2005 SC 281, discussed below.
5 12 October 2005, Lanark Sheriff Court, A492/05.

Over the following years a number of feus were granted out of the area affected by the deed of conditions, title to the pursuer's feu being registered in 2001. In the pursuer's feu disposition the deed of conditions was referred to for burdens, in the usual way, but it was not mentioned in the pertinents clause. Missing, therefore, was any statement to the effect that the subjects were conveyed 'together with the servitude specified in the deed of conditions aftermentioned'. As a result, no servitude was included by the Keeper in the property section of the title sheet. The defender, as the grantee of another feu, was owner of the putative burdened property (ie the 'public areas'). In this action the pursuer sought declarator as to the existence of the servitude and also interdict against obstruction by the defender.

The sheriff[1] held that its omission from the pertinents clauses of the feu disposition was fatal to the constitution of the servitude. The decision, however, was made in the context of an application for interim interdict and so without full citation and discussion of authorities. Further, on appeal the sheriff principal disagreed with the sheriff's view (albeit one which 'may well prevail at the end of the day') to the extent of finding that the pursuer had established a *prima facie* case which was sufficient for interim interdict; but as he accepted the sheriff's opinion that interim interdict should be refused on the balance of convenience, he did not express any firm view as to the merits.[2] In this note we are concerned only with the view expressed by the sheriff.

The sheriff's reasons for reaching his view were these (our lettering):[3]

[A] A Deed of Conditions has no named grantee. [B] A Feudal Superior could decide not to give certain purchasers rights contained in a Deed of Conditions. He might decide, in so far as he retains title to do so, to give an entirely different set of rights to particular purchasers. He might conclude that rights of access contained in a Deed of Conditions are not appropriate for a particular purchaser. A purchaser might negotiate a lower price on the basis that he is not to receive rights set out in a Deed of Conditions. There is no bar to any of that. In my judgment, if there is to be a grant to an individual of rights contained in a Deed of Conditions it follows that something more than the presence of a right in a Deed of Conditions is required. [C] A Deed of Conditions is quite a different creature to say a Disposition or a Deed of Servitude where there is a conveyance or grant to a named grantee. [D] *Halliday* deals with rights contained in a Deed of Conditions at page 300.[4] There it is said that a Deed of Conditions does not operate as a conveyance of the various common or other rights which it sets out and so when a disposition is being prepared of a portion of ground affected it is necessary to convey such rights expressly either by description *ad longum* or by reference to the Deed of Conditions. With that I respectfully agree.

Three arguments are advanced in this passage. With respect, all seem unsound. Thus, in the first place, it can hardly matter whether a deed has a grantee (parts [A] and [C]). If a deed of conditions can create real burdens (as

---

1 Sheriff Frank Pieri.
2 23 December 2005, Lanark Sheriff Court.
3 At para 31.
4 Ie J M Halliday, *Conveyancing Law and Practice* vol 2 (2nd edn 1997) para 33-74.

plainly it can), there can be no reason *in principle* why it should not be able to create servitudes as well.[1] Of course, the deed must then identify the benefited property in the servitude (in one sense, the grantee), but it is not suggested that there was a failure in this respect.[2]

The second argument (part [B]) has no bearing on the issue. Granters of deeds of conditions can change their minds. That is true even if a servitude has been created, because the granters will in that case own both the benefited and the burdened properties. Only if the benefited property has already been conveyed to someone else is it too late for granters to change their minds.

The final argument (part [D]) is based on a misunderstanding of the passage in Halliday. Professor Halliday is dealing with the case where a deed of conditions includes certain rights of common ownership. Naturally, rights of ownership cannot be transmitted by deed of conditions. For that a conveyance is required. So the rights in question must be included in the dispositive clause of the break-off dispositions. But a servitude is not a right of ownership. It does not need to be conveyed or appear in a conveyance. On the contrary, it can be created in a deed of any kind.[3] In principle it can be created in a deed of conditions.

But if the arguments deployed are unsound, it does not follow that the decision itself is wrong. There is indeed a difficulty in creating a servitude in a deed of conditions, but it is a different difficulty. In order for a servitude to come into existence, the benefited and the burdened properties must be in separate ownership, for no person can hold a servitude over his own property.[4] And since the granter of a servitude must own the burdened property (for otherwise he could not burden it), it follows that he must not also own the benefited property. In other words a servitude can only be created in favour of land which belongs to someone else.[5] As it happens, deeds of conditions usually attempt to create servitudes in favour of land owned by the granter – indeed in favour of the very land which is subject to the deed of conditions. That was the case in *Candleberry*.

There is a possible way out. Section 17 of the Land Registration (Scotland) Act 1979[6] provided that a land obligation specified in a deed of conditions becomes 'a real obligation affecting the land to which it relates' immediately on registration of the deed. A servitude is a type of land obligation. Section 17 could be expressly excluded in a deed of conditions and this was quite often done, but it was not done in *Candleberry*.

What effect does s 17 have on the rule that a person can only create a servitude in favour of land belonging to someone else? Three possibilities seem open.[7]

---

1 *Rubislaw Land Co Ltd v Aberdeen Construction Group Ltd* 1999 GWD 14-647, discussed in *Conveyancing 1999* pp 8–9.
2 In fact, as the sheriff points out (paras 42–46), the meaning of 'proprietor' in the grant of servitude gives rise to certain difficulties, which were to be founded by the defenders before the sheriff principal.
3 D J Cusine and R R M Paisley, *Servitudes and Rights of Way* (1998) para 6.22.
4 *Res sua nemini servit.*
5 *Hamilton v Elder* 1968 SLT (Sh Ct) 53.
6 Repealed with effect from 28 November 2004. For the current law, see below.
7 See also D J Cusine and R R M Paisley, *Servitudes and Rights of Way* (1998) para 2.07.

(1) The rule may be displaced by s 17, so that a servitude can indeed be created in a deed of conditions. (2) The rule may continue to stand, so that s 17 would apply where the benefited property was owned by a different person but not otherwise. (3) A third possibility is that the rule may be displaced partially but not fully, so that, while nothing is created at the moment of registration, the servitude is born as soon as ownership of the two properties is separated. It has never been decided which of these three interpretations of s 17 is correct.

Two factors reduce the impact of *Candleberry*, whatever the final decision in that case. First, few servitudes rest ultimately on a deed of conditions, for in practice the deed of conditions is usually followed by break-off conveyances in which the deed of conditions is referred to expressly. So even if not created by the deed of conditions, the servitude is created by the break-off conveyance; and the conveyance may effect the very separation of the properties which, previously, was the obstacle to creation. Of course, as the sheriff points out in *Candleberry*, the conveyance must refer to the deed of conditions in the right way. *Candleberry* concerned a conveyance of the benefited property, and in that case the reference, if it is to be effective to create a servitude, must be in the pertinents clause. But if it is the burdened property which is being conveyed, the deed must be referred to in the burdens clause. Importantly, *either is sufficient to create the servitude*. In other words, a servitude which is mentioned, but not created, in a deed of conditions is created on the first occasion on which it is properly referred to in a conveyance of either the benefited or the burdened property. In *Candleberry* the reference in the conveyance of the benefited property was faulty for the reason that the sheriff explained. But what seems to have been overlooked, at least at first instance,[1] is that – as so often in practice – the deed of conditions appears to have been referred to appropriately in the conveyance of the burdened property. For when the burdened property was conveyed to the defender in 2003, it seems that it was conveyed subject to the deed of conditions (including the servitude which the deed contained). If that is correct, it follows that the servitude was created, at latest, on registration of that conveyance in 2003. This is how many servitudes appear to have been created in the past.[2]

The second factor is that the problem is solved for the future by the Title Conditions (Scotland) Act 2003. Section 75(2) provides that:

> It shall be no objection to the validity of a positive servitude that, at the time when the deed was registered as mentioned in subsection (1) above, the same person owned the benefited property and the burdened property; but, notwithstanding section 3(4) of the 1979 Act (creation of real right or obligation on date of registration etc), the servitude shall not be created while that person remains owner of both those properties.

---

1 Something was made of the point in arguments before the sheriff principal.

2 See eg *Gray v MacLeod* 1979 SLT (Sh Ct) 17. It is true that the reference to the deed of conditions for burdens is likely to be qualified by words such as 'so far as still valid, subsisting and applicable' but, while this prevents the revival of burdens which were previously extinguished, it does not, it is thought, prevent the creation of burdens for the first time. Any other view would strike at the use of deeds of conditions not only for servitudes but for real burdens as well.

Whatever the position may have been under the old law, it is now clear that a servitude can be created in a deed of conditions.[1]

What words?

Since 28 November 2004 it has been necessary, in creating real burdens, to use the term 'real burden' or one of the terms specifying particular types of real burden, such as 'community burden' or 'conservation burden'. Otherwise the burden fails.[2] By contrast, there is no requirement to use the word 'servitude' in the creation of servitudes. Yet it is desirable to do so, because an unnamed obligation might be treated as merely personal and so as not binding successors.

In *Moss Bros Group plc v Scottish Mutual Assurance plc*,[3] discussed in our 2001 volume,[4] Lord Macfadyen took the, perhaps generous, view that the following obligation was a servitude:

> NOW in consideration of the reciprocal rights and obligations granted and undertaken herein Fairdale grants to Scottish Mutual a right of egress from the said subjects belonging to Scottish Mutual from the said openings to the public street over the said subjects belonging to Fairdale and Scottish Mutual grants to Fairdale a right of egress from the said subjects belonging to Fairdale from the said openings to the public street over the said subjects belonging to Scottish Mutual.

Not only was the word 'servitude' absent but the obligations were expressed as binding only the parties and not the parties and their successors. Nonetheless, taking the deed (a minute of agreement) as a whole, Lord Macfadyen decided that a servitude had been created.

A new case illustrates once again the difficulties in this area. In *Ord v Mashford*[5] a feu charter of 1932 provided that:

> And in respect that with the feuing of the piece of ground hereby disponed the field of Stanehead is as fully feued as it is desirable that the same should be feued, I hereby bind myself and my foresaids not to feu the unoccupied ground between the piece of ground hereby feued and Broughton Road, nor to allow the erection of buildings of any description thereon.

A dispute arose as to whether the closing words amounted to a servitude *non aedificandi*. In the opinion of the Lands Tribunal, they did not.[6] Perhaps surprisingly, given the context, it was said that the word 'foresaids' might mean

---

1 For the background to s 75(2), see Scottish Law Commission, Report on *Real Burdens* (Scot Law Com No 181, 2000; available on www.scotlawcom.gov.uk) para 12.21.
2 Title Conditions (Scotland) Act 2003 s 4(2)(a), (3).
3 2001 SC 779.
4 *Conveyancing 2001* pp 73–75.
5 2006 SLT (Lands Tr) 15. The Tribunal comprised Lord McGhie and I M Darling FRICS.
6 The decision, however, was *obiter* because the Tribunal, correctly, found that any servitude would have been extinguished by confusion.

successors as superiors of the land being feued rather than successors as owners of the field, and that this ambiguity undermined its effect.[1]

A comparison of the decisions shows the difficulty of advising clients on this matter. Only in the second case was there a reference to successors (by means of 'foresaids');[2] yet only in the first case was a servitude found to have been created.

For completeness it should be added that, under the Title Conditions Act, obligations *non aedificandi* must now be created as real burdens and not as servitudes; for it is no longer possible to create negative servitudes.[3]

Creation: implied servitudes

The facts of *McEwan's Exrs v Arnot*[4] concern two adjacent plots of land, both at one time the property of Mrs McEwan.[5] Originally Mrs McEwan lived in a house built on the plot nearest the road and known as Upper Mains. In the early 1990s she built a bungalow ('Tayview Cottage') on the second plot, and moved into it. Her intention was then to give Upper Mains to her son. But following a visit by her daughter, who lived in the USA, during the summer of 1993, she changed her mind and gave instructions to her solicitors to convey Upper Mains to her daughter. This was done. Tayview Cottage was, in effect, dependent on Upper Mains. Access from the road was only possible through Upper Mains, and all service connections – water, telephone and sewage – were by means of pipes, cables and a septic tank located in Upper Mains. Unfortunately none of this was mentioned in the disposition.

About a year later the house on Upper Mains burnt down. It seems that it was insured, and that the daughter was paid money on the policy, but the house was not restored. At some stage the daughter decided that her mother was not to make use of Upper Mains for access or services, other than pedestrian access. Accordingly, Mrs McEwan raised the present action against her daughter. (After the pursuer's death in January 2004, the action was continued by her executors.) There were two main craves. One was for declarator that Upper Mains was subject to the following servitudes in favour of Tayview Cottage:

---

1 At p 22G–I. The Tribunal laboured under the disadvantage of having only the excerpts from the deed which appeared in the burdens section of the title sheet of the putative benefited property. An inspection of the whole deed might have yielded a different result. For the difficulties here, and proposals for reform, see Scottish Law Commission, Discussion Paper on *Land Registration: Registration, Rectification and Indemnity* (Scot Law Com DP No 128, 2005; available on www.scotlawcom.gov.uk) paras 2.42 and 2.43.

2 The word 'foresaids' is tricky. One has to look carefully at who the 'foresaids' are. Sometimes they are 'heirs and assignees' or 'executors and assignees' neither of which may include singular successors. See G L Gretton, 'Heirs, executors and assignees: a conveyancing problem' (1984) 29 *Journal of the Law Society of Scotland* 103.

3 Title Conditions (Scotland) Act 2003 s 79.

4 7 September 2004, Perth Sheriff Court, A516/01. An appeal on a different point was refused by the sheriff principal on 11 February 2005.

5 The facts are taken from the pursuers' averments.

(a) a heritable and irredeemable right of access to and egress from the pursuer's subjects for pedestrian and vehicular purposes over the area shown delineated and hatched red on the plan subject to the obligation to maintain the said hatched area at equal expense along with the defender and her heritable successors;

(b) a heritable and irredeemable servitude right to use the mutual septic tank, the location of which is shown marked approximately 'EXISTING MUTUAL SEPTIC TANK' on the plan, and all connecting outflow pipes and other plant used in connection with the same in common with the defender and her successors, together with a right of access thereto for the purpose of inspection, maintenance, (including emptying) repair and renewal of the same subject to the obligation to meet the cost of such maintenance, repair and renewal at equal expense along with the defender and her successors; and

(c) a right to use all pipes, cables and other conduits required for the services of water supply, electricity supply and telecommunications services for the benefit of the pursuers' subjects over, through and under the defender's subjects hereinbefore referred to as the route of the same is shown approximately by a dotted line on the plan with a right of access thereto for the purpose of inspection, maintenance, repair and renewal subject to making good any damage caused thereby and subject to the obligation to maintain the same at equal expense along with the defender and her successors in so far as any of the same shall be mutual.

Of course no such servitudes had actually been included in the disposition granted in favour of the daughter, but it was argued that, nonetheless, such servitudes (including the maintenance obligations) could be implied.

The second crave, discussed elsewhere in this volume,[1] was for rectification of the disposition to the effect of inserting the missing servitudes.

The doctrine of implied servitude is the conveyancer's best friend. (The second-best friend is the doctrine of rectification.) Where servitudes are left out of a break-off disposition, it allows the argument that they are present by implication. Doubtless there are many cases in which implied servitudes have saved the Master Policy. In the present case, however, no professional negligence seems to have been involved,[2] for when Mrs McEwan asked her solicitors to convey Upper Mains she did not mention that she was living in the property immediately adjacent, still less that that property derived its services from Upper Mains. The titles would have been equally unhelpful to her solicitors because Upper Mains had been acquired at a different time from the property on which Tayview Cottage had come to be built.

---

1 See p 133.
2 D J Cusine and R R M Paisley, *Servitudes and Rights of Way* (1998) para 8.08: 'While a failure to make appropriate express provision for a servitude may be the basis of an action of professional negligence against a solicitor, nevertheless the omission may be the result of a lack of proper instruction on the part of the client in respect of the geographical location or make-up of the site in question.'

The relevant law is difficult and not entirely settled. An initial distinction is drawn between servitudes by grant and by reservation. In the present context, a servitude by implied grant would have been a servitude in favour of the daughter and Upper Mains. But what was being claimed was a servitude by implied reservation: in disponing Upper Mains to her daughter, so the argument went, Mrs McEwan must be taken to have reserved by implication certain servitudes to herself for the benefit of the property which she was keeping.

From Mrs McEwan's point of view it was unfortunate that the argument turned on implied reservation rather than implied grant, for it is harder to establish the former than the latter. This is because of the principle that a granter does not derogate from his grant, and must reserve expressly or not at all. How much harder is, however, unclear. In a leading English case, *Wheeldon v Burrows*,[1] Thesiger LJ stressed the non-derogation principle and seemed to confine implied servitudes by reservation to cases of necessity. This approach, however, is rejected by Sheriff Cusine and Professor Paisley in their definitive study of the modern law:[2]

> Despite indications favourable to its importation into Scotland in Bell's *Principles* and in two sheriff court cases, we are of the view that such a narrow approach is not part of Scots law, and that the weight of authority indicates that a party seeking to establish a servitude by means of a reservation implied from circumstances will require to demonstrate a greater degree of necessity than in relation to a grant implied from circumstances but he does not require to show absolute necessity.

We would agree with these remarks. Yet the case law – meagre as it is – is hardly encouraging, for in almost every case it which it has been pled, the argument based on implied reservation has failed. Typical is *Murray v Medley*[3] in which the sheriff held that access to mains water could not be regarded as 'necessary', and that accordingly where one building in a group was disponed with a water pipe which served the remaining buildings, no servitude could be implied. A century before that, a sheriff had reached an identical decision, citing Ulpian to the effect that '[a]ny servitude that a seller wishes to reserve for himself must be expressly reserved'.[4]

In the present case the sheriff allowed a proof before answer. There, it seems, the case ended, for we have heard the case settled on terms favourable to the pursuers. In making his decision, the sheriff showed at least provisional support for the approach taken by Cusine and Paisley:[5]

> If it is correct as Cusine and Paisley state that absolute necessity is not required, then something less, ie necessary for comfortable enjoyment, may indeed be a sufficient threshold.

---

1 (1879) 12 Ch D 31.
2 D J Cusine and R R M Paisley, *Servitudes and Rights of Way* (1998) para 8.19.
3 1973 SLT (Sh Ct) 75.
4 *Anderson v Handley* (1881) 2 Guthrie's Select Cases 532. The passage by Ulpian is from *Digest* 8.4.10.
5 At p 9.

Further, in the light of modern conditions, previous cases may no longer be a reliable guide. In relation to *Murray v Medley* the sheriff commented that:[1]

> I pause to consider whether these views would still be held today. It seems to me what is necessary may not be constant but may change with improved social conditions and that earlier case law has to be viewed with this caveat. It is at least arguable that in the 21st century the degree of necessity when considering services in the context of a dwellinghouse may have altered from the perception of former times.

In these words there may be the beginnings of a change of direction in the law. If so, it will bring servitudes by implied reservation closer to servitudes by implied grant. But it will not abolish the distinction. In our view the distinction is ripe for abolition. If Mrs McEwan had kept Upper Mains and disponed Tayview Cottage, and not the other way round, there could be little doubt that the relevant servitudes would have been implied, for in that case they would have been servitudes by implied grant. Yet there is no good reason of legal policy why the result should be different merely because the fact pattern was reversed. In fact it is often a matter of chance whether a particular separation comes about by grant or by reservation. If Anne is dividing her property and selling one half to Brian and the other half to Charles, it is arbitrary if the extent of implied servitudes should depend on which of the disponees happens to be first to register. Yet that is the current law: for if Brian registers before Charles, Brian will receive such servitudes over Charles' half as can arise by implied grant whereas in return Charles will only receive such servitudes (if any) as can arise by implied reservation.[2]

Creation: servitudes by acquiescence

It is sometimes said that a servitude can be created by acquiescence.[3] This rule, if it exists at all, is confined to those servitudes which involve significant construction work on the burdened property. Thus, if a person purports to initiate a servitude by extensive acts of construction on the land of a neighbour – for example, by building a septic tank or a reservoir or a metalled road – the neighbour may, if he knows of the acts and does not object, be personally barred from objecting later. On one view of the law the result is then to establish a servitude by acquiescence. In practice cases like this are uncommon, if only because, with time, a servitude which might have had its roots in acquiescence will become a servitude by prescription. At any rate, modern authority is lacking.

---

1 At p 9.
2 This is because, at the time when the first disposition is registered, one of the two halves is being granted (ie the half carried by that disposition) and so, necessarily, the other half is being reserved. What happens if both dispositions are registered simultaneously is unclear and shows the artificiality of the doctrine.
3 For a discussion, see D J Cusine and R R M Paisley, *Servitudes and Rights of Way* (1998) paras 11.37–11.46.

The issue arose in *Moncrieff v Jamieson*.[1] One of the arguments in favour of the alleged servitude in that case was that significant works had been carried out, without opposition, on the burdened property, with the result, it was said, that a servitude had been created by acquiescence. On the evidence the Extra Division was not satisfied that the works in question were sufficient,[2] and the case was decided on other grounds.[3] But the court expressed doubt as to whether acquiescence was a mode of creation at all. Of the numerous cases cited to the court, Lord Marnoch said that:[4]

> Having consulted all these authorities I am, however, of opinion that none go so far as to suggest that parties' actings can of themselves set up for the future a real right of praedial servitude.

Similarly, Lord Hamilton commented that 'the legal basis for the constitution of a real right of servitude by this mode is, in my view, very uncertain'.

While, however, we would share these doubts, it does not follow that acquiescence is irrelevant in this area. True, acquiescence cannot, probably, constitute a real right of servitude. But the neighbour who accepts an encroachment may often be personally barred from insisting on its removal or, it may be, from preventing its use.[5] And if the encroachment is obvious, or known about, a successor of that neighbour might be personally barred in turn. This last point, however, raises an issue in the law of encroachment which has never been properly resolved and where the position remains uncertain.[6]

Parking

The decision of the sheriff in the important case of *Moncrieff v Jamieson* was discussed in our 2003 volume.[7] The case has now been appealed to the Inner House where the decision of the sheriff was upheld by a 2:1 majority.[8] It is understood that there is to be a further appeal to the House of Lords.

The facts cannot be better introduced than by the sheriff:[9]

> In brief, this case involves a situation which has bitterly divided two sets of neighbours. The physical or geographical situation (ignoring the problems associated with access) can (in fair weather at least) be described as almost idyllic. The pursuers and the first and second defenders are young, nice-looking, married couples each with a young family. Both couples appear pleasant and intelligent and all were for long enough on reasonably good neighbourly terms with one another. The peace of that demi-Eden

---

1 [2005] CSIH 14, 2005 SC 281, 2005 SLT 225, 2005 SCLR 463.
2 It amounted only to the expenditure of £500 in laying hardcore.
3 As to which see below.
4 Paragraph 27.
5 In Lord Hamilton's view (para 85), that might well have been the position in *Moncrieff*.
6 K G C Reid, *The Law of Property in Scotland* (1996) para 176.
7 2004 SCLR 135, discussed in *Conveyancing 2003* pp 68–70.
8 [2005] CSIH 14, 2005 SC 281, 2005 SLT 225, 2005 SCLR 463.
9 2004 SCLR 135 at 164–165.

was shattered when almost out of the blue the defenders started to build a wall which intruded upon the access route to Da (ie 'the' in the Shetland dialect) Store and a turning place where the pursuers had been in the habit of turning or parking their cars. From that all else has followed.[1]

The dispute was between neighbours in Sandsound in Shetland. The pursuers had a number of craves, including declarator, interdict and damages. Property owned by the pursuers (Da Store) faced the sea and could be reached from the landward side only by a private road running through the third defenders' land.[2] At one time both properties had belonged to the same person, but the pursuers' property was broken off by a disposition in 1973. This conferred 'a right of access from the branch public road through Sandsound'. There was no dispute as to the pursuers' right to use the road itself, for it was accepted that the words were sufficient to create a servitude of way.[3] But a particular difficulty was caused by the fact that, due to a steep fall in the land, it was not possible to take a car from the end of the road on to the pursuers' property. Further, the road was too narrow for a vehicle to turn. Accordingly, the pursuers' practice was to use part of the defenders' land for turning and parking. For that purpose the pursuers added hardstanding. Matters proceeded amicably until 1998 when, as the sheriff mentioned, the defenders decided to build a wall taking in most of the turning area.

In the end, the dispute between the parties was a narrow one. It was accepted that the pursuers had a servitude of way over the road. It was further accepted that such a servitude was capable of carrying, by implication, certain ancillary rights, and that those rights included, in the present case, a right to use the defenders' land to load and unload and to turn. But what was disputed was whether there was also an ancillary right to park.[4] The sheriff had held that there was such a right and granted decree in favour of the pursuers. In the Inner House, however, the judges were in disagreement with one another.

Emphasising that servitudes must be strictly construed, Lord Hamilton was not prepared to regard parking as a necessary incident of the servitude of access. Parking was quite different in kind from loading and unloading, or turning. No doubt a right to park would be convenient in the present case. But if such a right was wanted, it could and should have been expressly granted in the 1973 disposition. As it happens, the factual background in 1973 hardly

---

1 There is something about this case which reaches the soul of the judiciary. In the Inner House, Lord Marnoch (at para 1) quoted the opening of the judgment by Donohue J in an almost identical case from Canada (*Lafferty v Brindley*, Ontario Supreme Court, 25 July 2001): 'Among its many charms Huron County boasts magnificent sunsets. If you look west from the plaintiffs' right of way along the lake bluff on a summer's evening the spectacle of the fiery orb sinking into the inland sea is sure to instil a sense of calm tranquillity. That feeling is an illusion! The very ground beneath your feet convulses in contending claims of adverse possession, prescriptive easement, and proprietary estoppel.'

2 However, since the case was before the sheriff a new public road has in fact been built to within metres of the pursuers' property, with a turning circle at its terminus.

3 Despite the fact that the word 'servitude' was not used. On this point see p 88 above.

4 An alternative argument, that a right to park had been established by acquiescence, was discussed above.

supported the idea that a right to park had been included by implication; for not only was there no indication that cars were using the road at that time, but the very idea of a servitude of parking was not then acknowledged as a part of the law of Scotland.

Lord Hamilton was, however, in a minority.[1] Both Lord Marnoch and Lord Philip were willing to imply a right to park. Lord Marnoch explained why:[2]

> [W]hile I recognise, and endorse, the principle that a grant of servitude must be strictly construed, that principle must on occasion yield to the competing principle that the grant of a right carries with it, by implication, what is necessary to the reasonable enjoyment of that right…. It is conceded – and, in my opinion, rightly conceded – by counsel for the appellants that in the circumstances of the present case the right of access in question must be construed, by implication, as including the right to turn and the right to load and unload goods and passengers. In my opinion, granted the particular location of the dominant property, the length of the access route in question and the nature of the terrain traversed by that route, it is quite simply unrealistic to draw a line between those implied rights and the entitlement of a visitor to park his vehicle for the duration of his visit which might extend over hours, nights, weeks or even months. And, once that be accepted, there is, in my opinion, no real distinction between what I have just described and a right on the part of the occupier to park for unlimited periods of time in connection with the reasonable use of the property. In short, I consider that any purchaser of the servient tenement as at 1973 would very readily have anticipated all of the foregoing rights as being necessary to the reasonable enjoyment of the dominant tenement. Questions of precisely how and where these rights are to be exercised, and how many vehicles can be parked, are questions which hopefully can be resolved by both parties acting sensibly but, if necessary, can be decided under reference to the test which I have just described and to the general rule that the proprietor of the dominant tenement must exercise his servitude right *civiliter*.

A number of points may be made about this decision. First, while the rule identified is capable of applying to any case in which a servitude of way is expressly granted – including to servitudes granted today, after the changes in the law effected by the Title Conditions (Scotland) Act 2003 – it is necessary to bear in mind that the facts of *Moncrieff* were unusual. In most cases of servitudes of way it is possible to park on the benefited property. If so, it is highly unlikely that the court would imply a right to park on the burdened property. There will not be many *Moncrieffs* in the future.

Secondly, and more importantly, the decision presupposes that, if a right to park had been expressed, such a right would have bound successors. In other words, the case establishes what had previously been in doubt, namely that parking can be created as a right which is ancillary to a servitude of way.

Thirdly, and conversely, the decision has nothing to say on whether a right to park can be created on its own, ie as a freestanding right unconnected with a right of way. Doubts were expressed on this point in a case decided in 2004,

---

1 At least one commentator, however, is persuaded by his analysis: see Ken Swinton, 'Parking again: *Moncrieff v Jamieson* 2005 CSIH 14' (2005) 73 *Scottish Law Gazette* 96.
2 Paragraph 24.

Nationwide Building Society v Walter D Allan Ltd,[1] but the matter has yet to be the subject of express decision. To some extent, of course, matters have been clarified by the Title Conditions (Scotland) Act 2003, which allows freestanding servitudes of parking if they are constituted by writing and registration.[2] But the Act is not retrospective, and does not in any event apply to servitudes created by other means, such as prescription.

Fourthly, like all servitudes a servitude of parking is subject to the restriction that it must not be repugnant with ownership – that is, that it must not be so extensive as to deprive the burdened owner of effective use of his land.[3] In the *Nationwide* case a servitude was denied on this basis. Nevertheless, it is doubtful whether servitudes of parking are more vulnerable to this objection than at least some other types of servitude.

Finally, although most countries (including England) draw their law of servitudes (or easements) from Roman law, making comparative research in this area especially fruitful, the court in *Moncrieff* was unwelcoming to authority from other jurisdictions. Thus Lord Marnoch chose to 'decline to derive any guidance from the Canadian law of easements' even although the case in question was very close on its facts,[4] while Lord Hamilton said that:[5]

> [A]lthough passing reference was made to certain authorities from England, I have not found these cases of assistance in determining the content of Scots law or in applying it to the circumstances of this case.

Usually in property law that is a sound approach, in respect of authority from England and other common law jurisdictions, but in the case of servitudes the common law jurisdictions can often give valuable assistance.

LEASES

Ambiguous clauses

Poorly drafted and ambiguous clauses can be found in contracts of every type. Commercial leases are no exception and 2005 produced two good examples.

Warren James Jewellers Ltd v Overgate GP Ltd

In recent years exclusivity clauses have been coming before the courts more frequently. In an exclusivity clause the landlord undertakes not to let out nearby

---

1 2004 GWD 25-539. For a discussion, see *Conveyancing 2004* pp 85–89.
2 Title Conditions (Scotland) Act 2003 s 76(1).
3 This common law rule has now been enacted, for express servitudes, as s 76(2) of the Title Conditions (Scotland) Act 2003.
4 *Lafferty v Brindley*. In fact Lord Marnoch reached the same result. In the course of his judgment he quoted (at para 1) from the decision in *Lafferty* at first instance (Ontario Superior Court of Justice, 25 July 2001), but it is assumed that counsel also cited the affirmation of that decision on 14 November 2003 by the Ontario Court of Appeal.
5 Paragraph 79.

premises to competitor businesses. For example, a company might take a lease in a shopping centre to trade as a wholefood store, and might wish to ensure that it was the only such shop in the centre. An exclusivity clause can either be absolute (no other such unit) or qualified (no more than a certain number of such units). Such clauses can be commercially vital to a tenant.

In *Warren James Jewellers Ltd v Overgate GP Ltd*[1] a unit in Dundee's Overgate Shopping Centre was held on a 15-year lease beginning in September 2000. The tenant, Warren James (Jewellers) Ltd, ran a jewellery business. The lease contained an exclusivity clause, whereby the landlord bound itself:

> 4.3 ... for so long as the said Warren James (Jewellers) Ltd is the Tenant under this Lease, not in respect of any first letting (which means the first time the Landlord lets the Lettable Unit in question and not in respect of any subsequent lettings) of any Lettable Unit to lease any such Lettable Unit (other than the Premises and two other Lettable Units only) with its Permitted Use having specified as its principal trade or business the retail sale of jewellery.

One day software may be available which will sound buzzers and flash lights when it finds a contract clause that is likely to result in litigation. If this clause were fed into such software, the computer would blow its fuses.

At the time (September 2000) there were already two other jewellery businesses in the centre. So did the clause mean (i) that the total allowable would be the existing two, plus the third to Warren James (Jewellers) Ltd? Or did it mean (ii) that after the lease to Warren James (Jewellers) Ltd the landlord would be limited to making two further leases to jewellery businesses, making a potential total of five? Actually these two possibilities are an oversimplification, because the exclusivity clause refers only to 'first lettings'. Because of that there was in fact no real cap on the number of jewellery businesses.

The landlord interpreted the clause in the second sense and, after September 2000, granted two further leases to jewellery businesses, thereby bringing the total number up to five. The tenant raised the present action, seeking declarator that the landlord was in breach of clause 4.3 and also seeking damages of £400,000. It claimed that since the competitors had begun trading, its own turnover had fallen substantially. In the end the Lord Ordinary agreed with the first interpretation, which was the one advanced by the pursuer.

Conveyancers traditionally like dive-in-and-hold-your-breath sentences. They feel that short sentences belong to Ladybird books. But long sentences, like long bits of string, easily get tangled. There is much to be learnt from Ladybird books.

City Wall Properties (Scotland) Ltd v Pearl Assurance plc[2]

The lease was of property at East Green Vaults under Aberdeen's Market Street. The property was a car park. The rent review clause provided that:

---

1 [2005] CSOH 142.
2 [2005] CSOH 137.

The rent so payable shall be subject to review at the instance of the Landlords at the relevant review date by addition per space of the product of 96 multiplied by 'the car park factor' (as hereinafter defined) applying at the relevant review date. For the purposes of the Lease 'the car park factor' shall mean the average of increased daily rates (ie the 9 hour rate from 0830 to 1730 hours charged to the public) at the Trinity Centre, Bon Accord Centre and the multi-storey College Street public car parks in Aberdeen....

It is reasonably clear what the intention must have been. The rent would be increased so as to track increases at the comparator car parks. But is this what the clause actually says? Does 'the car park factor' mean (i) the average *increase* at the comparator car parks, or (ii) the *total* new average rent at the comparator car parks? Thus suppose that the average comparator rate increased over the review period from £10 to £11. Would the 'car park factor' then be (i) £1 or (ii) £11? On the actual figures in the case, the first interpretation would have produced a new rental of £37,774, whereas the second would have produced a new rental of £64,083 – about 70% higher.

The case was first litigated in 2003 when it was held that the clause must be read literally, resulting in a rent which was absurdly high.[1] Thereafter the lessee was granted permission to amend its pleadings, and the case went back for a proof. After hearing evidence the Lord Ordinary found himself able to come to the opposite conclusion to the one he had reached before, and interpreted the clause in favour of the lessee. The lessee had also sought judicial rectification of the clause, but given the new decision the application for rectification was dismissed as unnecessary.[2]

Succession

The law about succession to leases is complex, both as to (i) who, if anyone, succeeds to the lease, and (ii) the procedural rules as to how this is to happen. Part of the complexity is because leases, like yoghurts in supermarkets, are of many different sorts. There are short leases and long leases, registered leases and unregistered leases, residential leases, commercial leases and agricultural leases. There are several different statutory regimes just for the various types of agricultural lease. Each type of lease tends to have its own set of succession rules. There seems to be nowhere in print where the practitioner can find a complete account of the law, though good starting points are Angus McAllister's *Scottish Law of Leases*[3] and Professor Meston's book on the Succession (Scotland) Act 1964.[4]

---

1 2004 SC 214, *Conveyancing 2003* Case (33).
2 For a brief account of the rectification aspects of the case, see p 19.
3 3rd edn 2002. Since that edition there have been further developments, in the shape of the Agricultural Holdings (Scotland) Act 2003, not to mention the arrival of same-sex partner's rights to succeed to some types of leases under the Civil Partnership Act 2004. See also Brian Gill, *The Law of Agricultural Holdings in Scotland* (3rd edn 1997).
4 M C Meston, *The Succession (Scotland) Act 1964* (5th edn 2002). This too is no longer quite up to date.

The Inner House case of *I & H Brown (Kirkton) Ltd v Hutton*[1] illustrates some of the difficulties.

The general rules

First, the general rules. These apply unless some special rule applies – which in practice it often will. The general rules are complicated enough in themselves, and the following account is a superficial one only.

At common law the lease passed to the heir, unless both (i) the lease allowed the tenant to bequeath, and (ii) the tenant did so. However, if the lease excluded all successors, whether *inter vivos* or *mortis causa*, the lease would come to an end (lapse) at the tenant's death. This last point is, however, not wholly free from difficulty.

The Succession (Scotland) Act 1964 did away with heirs, at least for most purposes, and so had to introduce a new set of general rules. The new rules are odd in a number of ways. Where a lease would, before 1964, have passed to the heir, since 1964 it has passed to one of a narrow class of persons, defined by s 16 of the 1964 Act as 'any one of the persons entitled to succeed to the deceased's intestate estate, or to claim legal rights or ... prior rights'. It is the executor who selects a person from this class.[2] A complication arises where the lease has an exclusion of assignation which is implied rather than express.[3] In that case the lessee has a limited power of bequest, namely to anyone in a narrow class, though apparently not quite the same narrow class.[4]

The 1964 Act assumes that a prohibition of assignation will be an absolute one and makes no provision for the common clause which prohibits assignation except with the landlord's consent, which consent will not be unreasonably withheld.[5]

The following table summarises the general rules, ie where some special statutory regime does not apply:

---

1 [2005] CSIH 66, 2005 SLT 885.
2 Naturally, the lease should first be confirmed to.
3 Why a contractual term should have a different *substantive* effect according to whether it is express or implied is puzzling.
4 Succession (Scotland) Act 1964 s 29. It is curious that the definition of the class is different from the one in s 16. It is 'any one of the persons who, if the tenant had died intestate, would be, or would in any circumstances have been, entitled to succeed to his intestate estate....' One of the odd aspects of this definition is that it includes every living person on our planet, for all human beings are related, and so everyone is (under some imaginable 'circumstances') the *haeres ab intestato* of everyone else. By contrast, the class defined in s 16 is limited to direct potential intestate successors. That is reasonably clear from the wording and was confirmed by *MacLean v MacLean* 1988 SLT 626. The same puzzle can be found in s 11 of the Agricultural Holdings (Scotland) Act 1991 (see below) and in subs (4B) of s 16 of the 1964 Act, as inserted by the Agricultural Holdings (Scotland) Act 2003.
5 Such clauses were rare in 1964.

	Prohibition of all successors[1]	Express prohibition of assignation	Implied prohibition of assignation	Assignation allowed
Testacy	Lapse	Executors can transfer to any member of a narrow class	To legatee, but only if member of a narrow class	To legatee
Intestacy	Lapse	Executors can transfer to any member of a narrow class	Executors can transfer to any member of a narrow class	Executors can transfer to any member of a narrow class

The executor has a year in which to transfer the lease. If he does not transfer it within that period the owner has the option to terminate the lease by giving notice to the executor. The notice period is not less than 12 months for agricultural property, but can be shorter for other types of property.[2] All this is general law only: the special statutory regimes modify it for particular kinds of leases.

Agricultural tenancies

A provision of particular importance is s 11 of the Agricultural Holdings (Scotland) Act 1991, which is extended to short limited duration tenancies and limited duration tenancies by s 21 of the Agricultural Holdings (Scotland) Act 2003.[3] This says that where there is a bequest of an agricultural tenancy to the tenant's 'son-in-law or daughter-in-law or to any one of the persons who would be, or would in any circumstances have been, entitled to succeed to the estate on intestacy by virtue of the Succession (Scotland) Act 1964' then the legatee has the option of intimating to the landlord, within 21 days of the death, that he accepts the bequest, in which case he becomes the tenant. There is in such a case no need for the executor to act. But if there is no s 11 intimation (or if there is such an intimation but the owner successfully objects to the legacy) then the case is dealt with under the 1964 Act.

I & H Brown (Kirkton) Ltd v Hutton

With that background sketched out, we return to the case of *I & H Brown (Kirkton) Ltd v Hutton*.[4] The pursuer was the owner of a farm. The defender, Mrs Hutton,

---

1 The law in this case seems to be the same as the pre-1964 common law, but, as mentioned above, the common law rule in this type of case is not wholly free from difficulty. However, such leases are rare.

2 *Sproat v South West Services (Galloway) Ltd* 2000 GWD 37-1416, discussed in *Conveyancing 2000* p 64, explores the precise meaning of this provision.

3 In this series we do not attempt to cover the law relating to agricultural tenancies, crofting tenure etc, so the text is by way of digression.

4 [2005] CSIH 66, 2005 SLT 885.

was in occupation. The question was whether she was the lawful tenant. Her father-in-law, Charles Hutton, had had a tenancy of the farm for many years. According to the defender, the tenancy had passed from him in 1990 to his son and the defender's husband, James Hutton, and then, on James' death, to her.[1] The pursuer's position was that the tenancy had never passed from Charles to James, and that when Charles died, in 1998, the tenancy came to an end.

By the time the case was litigated much of the documentation, including the lease itself, had been lost. One item that had survived was a letter from the landlord[2] to Charles in 1990:

> Following their recent meeting with you Messrs Davidson & Robertson have advised me that you have agreed that, with effect from Martinmas 1990, the rental of the above holding would be £1700 per annum on condition that your son James Stewart Hutton is taken into the lease. I confirm that the foregoing is acceptable to the Corporation, as Landlords, and should be pleased if you would sign one of the enclosed formal acceptances and return the same to me.

Charles had signed and returned this. To a large extent the case turned on the interpretation of this document. The defender's position was that James thereby became the sole tenant. The pursuer's position was that Charles and James became co-tenants and that when Charles died the statutory requirements were not complied with, with the result that the whole tenancy lapsed. The pursuer's argument was sustained by the sheriff, and on appeal the Inner House adhered to the sheriff's judgment.

The defender was a party litigant, and whilst she seems to have managed better than many such litigants, one may speculate whether a better case could have been made if she had had proper representation. Certainly the decision leaves a number of loose ends. Some of them are rather case-specific, while others are of more general interest. One case-specific point is how James is supposed to have become either co-tenant (according to the pursuer) or sole tenant (according to the defender). The 1990 letter was addressed only to Charles and there is no suggestion that James ever signed anything.

An issue of more general significance is the following. The pursuer's position, which was accepted by the court, was that after 1990 there was a co-tenancy between Charles and James. That being so, the pursuer's position, also upheld by the court, was that the whole tenancy then lapsed on Charles' death. Thus the sheriff says: 'As no steps were taken to confirm or transfer his interest in the lease as required by s 11 of the 1991 Act or s 16 of the 1964 Act, the whole lease terminated including the interest of James Hutton.' There is little discussion of this aspect of the case in the Inner House, possibly because the defender did not seriously challenge it. But one is left with the sense of unfinished business. Did Charles' death end the tenancy?

In the first place, the relevant legislation does not say that a lease ends *ipso facto* if it is not dealt with on the death of the tenant. It says that if there has been

---

1 How the tenancy passed to her is unclear from the decision.
2 At that time the British Coal Corporation.

no transfer within a year of the death then the landlord has the *option* of putting
an end to the lease. As already mentioned, the option is exercised by serving a
notice giving at least 12 months' warning. Perhaps the owner did exercise the
termination option, but, if so, that fact does not appear from the judgment.[1]

A second difficulty is as follows. It seems to have been assumed that where
there are two tenants, the lapse of the right of one of them will bring the whole
lease to an end. Perhaps that is so. It is true that difficulties would be involved
in either of the two alternatives, namely (i) that a half-lease continues, or (ii)
that the ongoing tenant becomes tenant of the whole lease. Nevertheless there
are two weighty arguments against the lapse of the whole lease. The first is
fairness. If X and Y are co-tenants, it seems unfair to Y if his right ends due
to delay by X's executor. The second is that s 16(3) of the 1964 Act authorises
the landlord to 'terminate the lease (in so far as it relates to the interest)'. The
words in brackets seem to mean that the effect of termination is limited to the
'interest' of the deceased.

In summary, the pursuer in this case had to get over two difficulties: (a) that
failure to dispose of a tenancy within a year of death does not lead to automatic
termination, and (b) that termination of a share of a lease may not mean
termination of the whole lease. It may be that these issues were addressed, but
if so the opinion issued by the Inner House does not seem to mention them.

The defender had an alternative line of argument. Although she took the view
that after 1990 James was the sole tenant, she argued that *esto* both Charles and
James were tenants, they were joint tenants rather than co-tenants. Because their
title was joint, the effect of Charles' death was that the whole tenancy vested
in the survivor, James. For a party litigant this was an ingenious argument. It
was, however, rightly rejected by the court, for joint property does not normally
exist outwith the context of trusts.

VARIATION AND DISCHARGE BY THE LANDS TRIBUNAL

Introduction

Until recently, the jurisdiction of the Lands Tribunal for Scotland to vary or
discharge real burdens and other 'land obligations' derived from ss 1 and 2 of the
Conveyancing and Feudal Reform (Scotland) Act 1970. The 1970 Act provisions
were repealed and replaced by the Title Conditions (Scotland) Act 2003 with
effect from 28 November 2004. The new provisions, which are quite extensive,
are to be found in part 9 (ss 90–104) of the 2003 Act. Valuable guidance as to their
application is given in the first decisions by the Lands Tribunal under the new
law: *George Wimpey East Scotland Ltd v Fleming*,[2] *Ord v Mashford*,[3] and *Church of*

---

1 What has just been said is true of all leases other than short limited duration tenancies and limited
  duration tenancies under the Agricultural Holdings (Scotland) Act 2003. With these the effect of
  non-transfer within a year of death is automatic termination.
2 2006 SLT (Lands Tr) 2. The Tribunal comprised J N Wright QC and A R MacLeary FRICS.
3 2006 SLT (Lands Tr) 15. The Tribunal comprised Lord McGhie and I M Darling FRICS.

Scotland General Trustees v McLaren.[1] *Ord* is of particular significance and is likely to be relied on for many years to come. We quote extensively from it below.

Some background seems necessary. One result of the 2003 Act[2] has been a proliferation of enforcement rights in respect of real burdens. Whereas, formerly, a burden might have been enforceable by the feudal superior alone, today it may be enforceable by the 10 – or 100 – neighbours whose titles share the same conditions.[3] In such cases, consensual discharge by minute of waiver is obviously impossible. Admittedly, if the burden in question is more than 100 years old, the 2003 Act introduces a new 'sunset rule' by which burdened owners can take matters into their own hands and procure a discharge by service and registration of a notice of termination.[4] But if a burden is less than 100 years old, the only means of having it removed may be an application to the Lands Tribunal. As before, the Tribunal's jurisdiction is not confined to real burdens but applies to all 'title conditions', including servitudes and conditions in long leases.

Opposed and unopposed applications

A decision to apply to the Lands Tribunal will be influenced by the likelihood of opposition. If the application is opposed, a hearing must take place and the different arguments weighed. The process is potentially lengthy and the result uncertain. But an unopposed application must be granted by the Tribunal without further enquiry, provided (with some exceptions) it is concerned with real burdens.[5] That is a change in the law. It means that an unopposed application in respect of real burdens cannot fail. And the process, more administrative in nature than judicial, is relatively quick and cheap: a fee of £238 is payable to the Tribunal,[6] to which must be added legal fees and advertising and other expenses.

Under the previous law around 50% of applications were unopposed.[7] It is too early to know whether this figure will be maintained under the new law. As already mentioned, the tendency of the 2003 Act is to increase the number of potential enforcers.[8] On the other hand, opposition now involves payment

---

1 2006 SLT (Lands Tr) 27. The Tribunal comprised J N Wright QC and I M Darling FRICS.
2 And especially s 53 of that Act.
3 Of course even under the old law, neighbours often had enforcement rights, whether conferred expressly or by implication. But this was easy to overlook.
4 Title Conditions (Scotland) Act 2003 ss 20–24. See further *Conveyancing 2003* pp 120–121.
5 Title Conditions (Scotland) Act 2003 s 97. Facility burdens (typically burdens in respect of common maintenance) and service burdens are excluded.
6 This comprises an application fee of £150 and a further fee of £88 for making the order. See items 17 and 21 in sch 2 of the Lands Tribunal for Scotland Rules 1971, SI 1971/218, as amended in particular by the Lands Tribunal for Scotland Amendment (Fees) Rules 2003, SSI 2003/521, and the Lands Tribunal for Scotland Amendment (Fees) Rules 2004, SSI 2004/480.
7 Scottish Law Commission, Report on *Real Burdens* (Scot Law Com No 181, 2000; available on www.scotlawcom.gov.uk) para 6.3.
8 This is done both by increasing the number of benefited properties, and also by extending enforcement rights from owners to tenants, proper liferenters and non-entitled spouses. But only representations by the owner count for the purposes of giving an application the status of being opposed: see Title Conditions (Scotland) Act 2003 s 97(3)(a).

of a modest fee (currently £25)[1] and, more importantly, may attract liability for expenses. Under the former law those whose opposition was unsuccessful were not normally liable for more than their own expenses. The applicant's expenses were a matter for the applicant. Under the 2003 Act, by contrast, expenses will normally follow success, so that unsuccessful opponents will have to meet the expenses of both sides.[2]

One category of opponent is missing from the new law. Under the 1970 Act the Tribunal had a discretion to accept representations from interested parties – typically neighbours – who were affected by the application but were not themselves entitled to enforce the burden.[3] In practice such 'affected persons' were often heard. They cannot be heard under the 2003 Act. In *Ord v Mashford*, the Tribunal was sanguine as to the loss:[4]

> Under the 2003 Act there is no place for affected persons. Although this might appear to be a significant change, it must be recognised that affected persons had no 'rights' under the 1970 Act. The tribunal could consider their views. We might give considerable weight to them if this appeared to fall within the intention of the obligation. Frequently, however, they added little to the process.... [Under the 2003 Act] these owners have no right to any say in the matter. As members of the public they, of course, had, and have, the right to try to preserve the perceived amenity of their property by objecting to unsuitable development. Any such objections would be taken into account by the planning authority as part of their assessment of matters in the public interest.

Opposed applications: statutory criteria

Where an application is opposed, a hearing takes place and there is a site visit, as under the previous law. But the statutory criteria have changed.

Under the 1970 Act[5] the Lands Tribunal could grant an application only

> on being satisfied that in all the circumstances,
> (a) by reason of changes in the character of the land affected by the obligation or of the neighbourhood thereof or other circumstances which the Tribunal may deem material, the obligation is or has become unreasonable or inappropriate; or
> (b) the obligation is unduly burdensome compared with any benefit resulting or which would result from its performance; or
> (c) the existence of the obligation impedes some reasonable use of the land.

Under the 2003 Act reasonableness is directed neither at the burden (category (a) above) nor at the intended use of property which the burden obstructs

---

1 Item 23 in sch 2 of the Lands Tribunal for Scotland Rules 1971, SI 1971/218, as inserted by the Lands Tribunal for Scotland Amendment (Fees) Rules 2004, SSI 2004/480.
2 Title Conditions (Scotland) Act 2003 s 103(1).
3 Conveyancing and Feudal Reform (Scotland) Act 1970 s 2(2).
4 At pp 22L–23B.
5 Conveyancing and Feudal Reform (Scotland) Act 1970 s 1(3).

(category (c)). Rather the question for the Tribunal is whether 'it is reasonable to grant *the application*'.[1] In reaching its decision, the Tribunal is directed to have regard to the factors set out in s 100. Unlike the categories in the 1970 Act, these factors are cumulative and not alternative.

The factors set out in s 100 are the following:

(a) any change in circumstances since the title condition was created (including, without prejudice to that generality, any change in the character of the benefited property, of the burdened property or of the neighbourhood of the properties);

(b) the extent to which the condition –

   (i) confers benefit on the benefited property; or
   (ii) where there is no benefited property,[2] confers benefit on the public;

(c) the extent to which the condition impedes enjoyment of the burdened property;

(d) if the condition is an obligation to do something, how –

   (i) practicable; or
   (ii) costly,

   it is to comply with the condition;

(e) the length of time which has elapsed since the condition was created;

(f) the purpose of the title condition;

(g) whether in relation to the burdened property there is the consent, or deemed consent, of a planning authority, or the consent of some other regulatory authority, for a use which the condition prevents;

(h) whether the owner of the burdened property is willing to pay compensation;

(i) if the application is under section 90(1)(b)(ii) of this Act, the purpose for which the land is being acquired by the person proposing to register the conveyance; and

(j) any other factor which the Lands Tribunal consider to be material.

The change, however, is perhaps more of form than of substance. Certainly that is the view taken by the Lands Tribunal in *Ord v Mashford*:[3]

> The approach of the tribunal under the 1970 Act was complicated by the apparent need to make a finding that the circumstances fitted into one of the categories (a), (b) or (c) of section 1(3) before taking the discretionary decision as to whether the obligation should be removed. This led to a raft of case law analysing particular situations and their place within the statutory structure. But the tribunal evolved a method of dealing with category (c) which came close to the approach which now falls to be taken under section 100. Although that category might have appeared to require the tribunal first to identify a reasonable use and then to consider whether such use justified the exercise of the broad discretion to vary or discharge, the tribunal recognised that the 'reasonableness' of a particular use could not be decided in abstract. This view

---

1 Title Conditions (Scotland) Act 2003 s 98.
2 Ie in the case of a personal real burden such as a conservation burden.
3 2006 SLT (Lands Tr) 15 at pp 19L–20D.

was supported by the Inner House: *Murrayfield Ice Rink Ltd v Scottish Rugby Union*[1] (at page 29). To decide whether a proposed use was reasonable the tribunal had to have regard to all the circumstances. Once a decision was reached that a case fell within section 1(3)(c) there was little scope for exercise of any further discretion: see *Railtrack v Aberdeen Harbour Board*.[2] So, in practice, the tribunal decided whether it was reasonable to discharge an obligation having regard to any circumstances it considered material. Examples of factors considered material could be found in the decided cases but, as the tribunal would take into account any factor which it thought relevant to particular circumstances, the guidance from previous decisions was not exhaustive.

The new Act adopts a similar approach. It requires the tribunal to assess reasonableness. It assists litigants by identifying a list of factors which can be expected to be significant but makes it clear that the range of factors which might be relevant is not limited. Decisions on the reasonableness of removal of a benefited party's legal rights may still involve a difficult exercise of discretion but the approach can be expected now to be more straightforward. Decisions will be seen more clearly to turn on the analysis and weighing of fact rather than on comparison with previous cases.

In *Ord* the Tribunal thought it 'unlikely that there could be many situations where the change of Act would make a difference in substance'.[3] Similarly, in the slightly earlier case of *George Wimpey East Scotland Ltd v Fleming*, a differently composed Tribunal said that '[i]t is not apparent that they [the new provisions] will lead to any change in substance from the way in which the previous provisions were applied by the Tribunal over many years'.[4] However, these statements may under-estimate the significance of the changes. And even if the legislation had been unchanged, the mere fact that superiors have been replaced by neighbours, who will often have a solid interest in resisting discharge, is likely to affect the success rate of applications.

Applying section 100

The new cases, and especially *Ord v Mashford,* are instructive as to how the factors in s 100 are likely to be applied. The proper approach, it is said, is not to consider each head in turn and ask whether the application succeeds or fails under that head. That was the approach of the old law. Under the new law the factors are cumulative rather than alternative and fall to be considered together.[5] No significance is to be given to the order in which the factors happen to be listed in s 100. In fact, the Tribunal emphasised, they are of unequal importance.

---

1 1973 SC 20.
2 17 December 2001; available on www.lands-tribunal-scotland.org.uk/records.html.
3 At p 19L.
4 2006 SLT (Lands Tr) 2 at p 10F. In that case the Tribunal actually applied both sets of provisions and reached the same result.
5 *George Wimpey East Scotland Ltd v Fleming* at pp 10L–11A. This passage was quoted with approval in *Ord v Mashford* at p 20H.

Perhaps the most important, and certainly the one with which any discussion should begin, is factor (f) (the purpose of the condition).[1] According to the Tribunal:[2]

> We are satisfied that the purpose of the title condition [factor (f)], if it can be identified, will tend to carry weight. It will always be likely to be of greater significance than, say, the length of time which has elapsed since the obligation was first imposed [factor (e)]. If the original purpose can still be achieved, the period of time which has elapsed may be of little significance. On the other hand, if the original purpose can no longer be achieved, the time may be a very minor consideration. Purpose is also of considerable importance in attempting to assess the significance of evidence of change of circumstances [factor (a)]. Change will be of little weight unless it can be shown to be relevant to the obligation. Reference to purpose or intention will also play a part in weighing the impact of removal of the obligation [factor (b)].

In *Ord v Mashford* the Tribunal gave helpful indications as to its likely approach to a number of the statutory factors:

Factor (a): change in circumstances

The equivalent provision in the 1970 Act gave prominence to 'changes in the character … of the neighbourhood'. Neighbourhood in factor (a) is relegated to the end, where it appears as one of a non-exhaustive list of things that might have changed. The Tribunal regards the change as both significant and helpful:[3]

> We are satisfied that in the context of the scheme of section 100(a) it is unnecessary and inappropriate to approach change by seeking first to determine the extent of the neighbourhood. If change in a local area is relevant we can take it into account without the need to characterise it in any particular way. Indeed, an illustration of the simplification afforded by the new Act can readily be found in relation to the question of change in the 'neighbourhood'. Certain *dicta* under the old Act had given rise to the understanding that in every case based on section 1(3)(a) it was necessary to identify or define the 'neighbourhood' as a first step. Only once it was known what the 'neighbourhood' was, could it be decided whether there had been relevant changes. This gave rise to a great deal of examination, cross-examination and debate. However, this can now be seen as essentially sterile material. Even under the 1970 Act the critical issue was whether there had been relevant change. A physical change having a bearing on a view might well be described as a change in the neighbourhood even if it was at some distance from the benefited subjects. On the other hand, if the relevant issue was protection of quiet or light, the focus would necessarily be on a much smaller area.

---

1 *Ord v Mashford* at p 23I. This factor did not appear at all in the original list as prepared by the Scottish Law Commission.
2 *Ord v Mashford* at p 20J.
3 *Ord v Mashford* at p 24E–G.

Factor (b): extent of benefit to benefited property

In the Tribunal's view, factor (b) is of considerable importance, unlike its predecessor provision in the 1970 Act.[1] In particular, the Tribunal emphasised that:[2]

> Although it may appear that this factor is essentially a repetition of section 1(3)(b) of the 1970 Act, we think it important to recognise that it plays a completely different role in the context of assessment for the purposes of section 98. Under the old provision it was used in the context of a balance of 'undue' burden against benefit. It was well established that little benefit was needed to persuade the Tribunal that an application under that section should be refused: see, for example, *Stevens v Smith*.[3] Now, factor (b)(i) will have a major role as being likely to be the main, if not the sole factor pointing against the grant of an application. *But for this factor, it would normally be reasonable to discharge the condition.*[4] As discussed above, factor (f) may have an important supporting role in this part of the assessment but identification of the present benefit is fundamental.

General benefit is different from the question of interest to enforce (which can relate only to a particular breach), and the latter is not relevant to an application for variation and discharge.[5]

In the Tribunal's view, benefit must be viewed in the light of the purpose of the condition – which in turn (see below) is interpreted subjectively, by reference to the intention of the original parties. If, *in fulfilment of that purpose*, the burden confers benefit, that is a matter which properly falls within factor (b). But if the burden confers only *benefit of a different kind*, that benefit is disregarded for the purposes of factor (b).[6] Whether this approach is within the letter and spirit of s 100(b) is perhaps open to question. In some cases it will lead to the removal of good and useful burdens which now serve a purpose other than that which was originally intended.

Factor (c): extent to which enjoyment of burdened property impeded

Perhaps surprisingly, the Tribunal treats factor (c) as unimportant. It is self-evident that enjoyment is impeded, for otherwise no application would have been brought. But that is a reason for the application rather than a reason why it should be granted:[7]

> [W]e do not think this a factor which can be expected to carry much weight. It must not be forgotten that the burden must have been accepted, initially, as part of a negotiated

---

1 The predecessor provision, s 1(3)(b) of the Conveyancing and Feudal Reform (Scotland) Act 1970, read: 'the obligation is unduly burdensome compared with any benefit resulting or which would result from its performance'.
2 *Ord v Mashford* at p 24K–L.
3 16 May 1997; available on www.lands-tribunal-scotland.org.uk/records.html.
4 Our emphasis.
5 *Church of Scotland General Trustees v McLaren* 2006 SLT (Lands Tr) 27 at para 34.
6 *Church of Scotland General Trustees v McLaren* at para 39.
7 *Ord v Mashford* at p 25L.

arrangement. The applicants, of course, bought the land at a price which reflected the existence of a restriction.

This can be criticised both for the argument and for the result to which it leads. The argument seems not to correspond with ordinary experience, for burdens are frequently created without negotiation, and often – being derived from a standard style – without much consideration for their relevance to the circumstances in question. In many cases (though not of course in all), the price paid by a subsequent acquirer is unaffected by the presence of restrictions. (If it is affected, this would be a ground for compensation in the event that the burden was discharged.[1]) As to result, it seems likely that factor (c) was intended to be balanced particularly against factor (b) and that both must be given proper weight. The question to be asked is whether the burden outweighs the benefit. If it does, the burden should normally be discharged – if necessary subject to the payment of compensation. Something of this approach can be seen in the Report of the Scottish Law Commission in which the provisions were first set out. According to the Commission, 'a consideration of the benefit conferred on one property [ie factor (b)] must be balanced by a consideration of the burden imposed on the other [ie factor (c)]'.[2] Neither factor is decisive on its own:[3]

> Of course a condition should not be discharged *only* because it imposes a substantial impediment on the burdened property. The condition may be recent. Nothing may have changed since it was first imposed. Substantial impediment to the burdened property may be balanced, or even outweighed, by substantial advantage to the benefited property.

But, by inference, if the balance of argument is the other way around – if, in other words, impediment outweighs advantage – the burden should usually be discharged.

Factor (e): age of condition

The Tribunal regards this factor as usually unimportant:[4]

> [M]ere duration tells us little as to whether it [the condition] can be regarded as out of date, obsolete or otherwise inappropriate. At first blush, therefore, there might be little weight to attach to this factor. One possible effect of this provision is to direct attention

---

1 Title Conditions (Scotland) Act 2003 s 90(6), (7)(b).
2 Scottish Law Commission, Report on *Real Burdens* (Scot Law Com No 181, 2000; available on www.scotlawcom.gov.uk) para 6.76.
3 Report on *Real Burdens* para 6.77.
4 *Ord v Mashford* at pp 25L–26A. A slightly greater role was conceded in *Church of Scotland General Trustees* at para 42: 'As it seems to us, this will often be a factor of much less significance than the purpose of the condition, although sometimes the fact of very recent creation may tell with some strength against the application. However, this is unquestionably a very old condition, which was conceived in very different circumstances and which may be said long ago to have fulfilled its purpose.'

to the need to have regard to the impact of gradual change in attitudes over time. We have attempted to give some expression to this element in our discussion under (a) above and need not repeat it.

By contrast, the Scottish Law Commission ascribed to age a more significant role:[1]

A recent condition deserves the benefit of the doubt, particularly if the original parties remain in place. But a condition which has already burdened the land for many years has perhaps run its course. The reasonable expectations of the parties have been fulfilled. The Tribunal should hesitate before it agrees that the land should be burdened for a further period.

The scheme of the Act rather supports this view. If a burden is more that 100 years old, it is subject to unilateral discharge under the sunset rule.[2] If it was created within the last 100 years but is still quite elderly, that is a factor which is favourable to its discharge by the Lands Tribunal.

Factor (f): purpose of condition

The key role to be given to this factor has already been mentioned. Importantly, the Tribunal appears to interpret it historically and subjectively. The question is not 'what purpose does the condition now achieve?' but rather 'what purpose did the original parties wish it to achieve'? Often this will bring in factor (a), for the most likely reason for failure of purpose is a change in circumstances. This approach disregards the present value of a condition if that value does not reflect the purpose which was originally intended. That in turn makes discharge more likely.

An obvious problem with this approach is the difficulty of discerning the parties' intentions many years after the event. In practice the only evidence will often be the deed itself, and, unless the deed is clear on the point, assumptions as to purpose are at risk of being ill informed and speculative.[3]

Factor (g): planning and other consents

The approach to planning consent under the former law was explained by the Tribunal as follows:[4]

In the early cases under the 1970 Act, stress was often laid on the fact that planning consent had been given. In some cases much time was taken in exploration of the planning process. However, it was recognised that planning was primarily concerned with reasonableness in the public interest. Properly understood, reference in the older cases to a grant of planning consent as persuasive was frequently to be seen as

---

1 Scottish Law Commission, Report on *Real Burdens* para 6.79.
2 Title Conditions (Scotland) Act 2003 ss 20–24.
3 It may be noted in this connection that in *Church of Scotland General Trustees v McLaren* the Tribunal rejected an argument partly because (para 46) 'it involves an assumption as to the original granter's intention'.
4 *Ord v Mashford* at p 21B–C.

equivalent to no more than that the use proposed would be accepted as reasonable from the viewpoint of the general public.

Reasonableness of use is no longer an issue under the new law, and for this or other reasons the Tribunal regards the fact that planning permission has been granted as, generally, a neutral factor.[1] By contrast, the Scottish Law Commission saw it as helpful, as least in a modest way, to the case of the applicant.[2]

Factor (h): whether the owner of the burdened property is willing to pay compensation

The Tribunal is uncertain as to the role of this factor:[3]

> It is not clear what role willingness to pay compensation is expected to play in the overall assessment. It may be assumed in every case that an applicant is prepared to pay such compensation as may be determined by the Tribunal and we would not expect to hear evidence of this.

Traditionally, the Tribunal made a clear distinction between the merits of an application and the question of whether compensation should be paid, and that distinction seems to be maintained under the new law. Compensation is relevant only where the application is successful on the merits. Yet factor (h) (which was not part of the Scottish Law Commission's proposals) rather suggests that the distinction should be abandoned. In other words, if the applicant is willing to pay compensation, the suggestion seems to be that the Tribunal should be more inclined to find for the applicant on the merits.

Factor (j): any other factors

As under the previous law, the Tribunal is able to take other factors into account, although those specially listed will often amount to all the relevant circumstances. One factor which is plainly *not* relevant, however, is the personal circumstances of those who happen, for the moment, to be owners of properties in question. The Tribunal's position on this point is clear from *Ord v Mashford*:[4]

> For completeness we confirm that under the 1970 Act it was well established that the tribunal was concerned with matters of heritable rights and not with purely personal interests. Regard was focused on the attitudes of typical proprietors and the particular interests of individual applicants and respondents were regarded as irrelevant. Had there been any intention to change this approach, reference to personal circumstances would, we think, have been set out explicitly as a factor under section 100. Under the new provisions, as they stand, for example, we think it appropriate to continue to give no weight to purely personal matters.

---

1 *Ord v Mashford* at p 26D.
2 Scottish Law Commission, Report on *Real Burdens* paras 6.80–6.82.
3 *Ord v Mashford* at p 26E.
4 *Ord v Mashford* at p 21E.

In *Church of Scotland General Trustees v McLaren* the Tribunal declined to take account of evidence that the burdened property could still be used for a purpose similar to that which the burden sought to achieve (a church or lay training centre) rather than, as the applicants intended, for housing. The reasoning was that:[1]

> [T]his jurisdiction (like the 1970 Act jurisdiction) involves the entitlement of an owner of property to make use of his property. It enables private title conditions to be lifted, on a test of reasonableness, so as to prevent benefited proprietors from either extracting a ransom or hindering reasonable uses of property. It does not give a benefited proprietor any new positive right of control over the use of the property, except so far as necessary to further legitimate purposes still protected by the obligation. The benefited proprietor's own view as to how the property should be used is, of itself, irrelevant. Equally, any view which the Tribunal may hold as to how the property should be used would not be directly relevant.

Of course, evidence as to alternative uses is likely to have a bearing on factor (c) (extent to which condition impedes enjoyment of the property), for a condition which allows a number of different uses impedes enjoyment less than one which does not. But that is not the same as evidence that the property could be used for a particular purpose which is selected by the benefited proprietor.

The decisions themselves

In all three cases the applicant for variation or discharge was successful, although in two the Tribunal left open the possibility that the benefited owner might apply for compensation. Something can be learned from each case.

In *George Wimpey East Scotland Ltd v Fleming*[2] the application was for variation of the route of a servitude of way. The decision suggests that such applications may often be viewed with favour.

In *Ord v Mashford*[3] – the only case of the three in which there might have been grounds for hesitation – the Tribunal took a robust view on the question of benefit (factor (b)). The benefited property enjoyed an open outlook over a field, by virtue of a 1938 servitude which forbade any building on the field. The applicant wished to build a single-storey house. In the Tribunal's opinion, a view over open land was not necessarily better than one over a house. That depended both on the land and on the house:[4]

> The field might be left to become overgrown. It might be used for a non-agricultural purpose which did not involve building. Residents might or might not be happy, for example, with a conifer plantation but such a development would completely change the nature of the amenity presently enjoyed. Use of the land for any form of public recreation would change things in a different way. On the other hand, a house with normal level of attention to garden care would preserve many aspects of the amenity currently enjoyed.

---

1 *Church of Scotland General Trustees v McLaren* at para 46.
2 2006 SLT (Lands Tr) 2.
3 2006 SLT (Lands Tr) 15.
4 *Ord v Mashford* at p 25B.

Matters would be different, the Tribunal conceded, if a block of flats were proposed. But the current proposal would 'not have any great adverse impact'. Accordingly, the burden should be varied to allow a house to be built.

An oddity in *Ord* is that the benefited owners held their house on a different title from the bulk of their garden and that, strictly, only the latter was the benefited property in the burden. Nonetheless, apparently by agreement, the Tribunal decided the case as if the benefited property was the house.[1]

Finally, the decision in *Church of Scotland General Trustees v McLaren*[2] suggests that the fact that a burden was originally created in a grant in feu may make it easier to obtain a discharge. This is partly to do with the nature of superiorities and partly because the Tribunal, perhaps controversially,[3] has chosen to tie benefit (factor (b)) to purpose (factor (f)). Burdens in feu grants did not necessarily confer benefit on particular (physical) properties but might be concerned with larger questions of public interest. The burden in the *Church of Scotland* case was indeed an example, requiring the property to be used for the site of a church. But a burden which has a public purpose may not confer benefit on the property to which, following feudal abolition, enforcement rights have now been attached; or rather any benefit which it does confer is likely to be unrelated to the public purpose of the burden and so, according to the Tribunal, falls to be disregarded as adventitious. In the *Church of Scotland* case the burden had the effect in practice of preserving the amenity of the neighbouring property. That was why its owner had taken the trouble to acquire the superiority and reallot the burden by registration of the appropriate notice.[4] Nonetheless, according to the Tribunal the only relevant question was whether the public purpose of providing a church conferred particular benefit on the property which happened to be next door. The answer, unsurprisingly, was no.[5]

Use of prior case law

Tribunal jurisprudence will clearly be important for fleshing out the new law on variation and discharge. *Ord v Mashford*,[6] in particular, is a case which is likely to be cited by every applicant for years to come. But as the Tribunal says in *Ord*:[7]

> Even under the 1970 Act our experience had been that while a grasp of case law helped parties to understand the approach taken by the Tribunal to the inter-related provisions of section 1(3), the detail of previous decisions was seldom of assistance in the direct assessment of reasonableness.
>
> One reason why reference to apparently similar previous cases tended to provide little real assistance is that it has been the experience of the Tribunal that a site inspection

---

1 *Ord v Mashford* at p 23F–G.
2 2006 SLT (Lands Tr) 27.
3 See above.
4 Ie under the Abolition of Feudal Tenure etc (Scotland) Act 2000 s 18.
5 *Church of Scotland General Trustees v McLaren* at para 39.
6 2006 SLT (Lands Tr) 15.
7 *Ord v Mashford* at p 20D–F.

plays a significant part in many decisions. Even with the benefit of hearing oral evidence and studying maps, plans and photographs, the Tribunal has often been influenced by the impression derived on site. That element cannot readily be assessed from the text of reported decisions. Litigants seeking to make comparisons with previous cases usually do so without the benefit of plans and photographs. While broad guidance to our approach under the new Act will, we hope, be derived from our decisions as they emerge, we think it likely that attempts to rely on apparently close factual comparison will seldom be worthwhile.

This may overstate matters. Although not precedents in the normal sense, past decisions will often be a useful guide to future decisions. If, for example, the Tribunal regularly allows an alteration in the route of a servitude – as it did in *George Wimpey East Scotland Ltd v Fleming* – it is reasonable to suppose that it will do so again. And even if extensive citation of decisions is unwelcome to the Tribunal, and likely to be discouraged, the decisions will continue to be of value in advising clients as to the prospects of success.

STANDARD SECURITIES

Standard securities are often granted for the debts, not of the granter personally, but of a business in which the granter has an interest. And such cases often give rise to difficulties. *AIB Group (UK) plc v Guarino*[1] and *Bank of Scotland v Forman*[2] are examples.

Due and resting owing?

In *AIB Group (UK) plc v Guarino*[3] the defender granted a guarantee to the pursuer for the debts of a company. He also granted to the pursuer a standard security. Neither deed is quoted in the judgment, but it seems likely that the standard security contained an obligation to pay on demand all sums due or to become due.

The pursuer served a calling-up notice[4] on the defender and then raised an action seeking declarator of its right to take possession and sell, in which it was eventually successful. Though such actions (which must be distinguished from s 24 applications)[5] are common, the actual wording seldom finds its way into print, so it may be of interest to quote the sheriff's interlocutor, reflecting the terms of the crave in the writ. The sheriff:

(1) Finds and declares that the defender granted a Standard Security in favour of the pursuers registered in the Land Register of Scotland under Title Number GLA 93561 on

---

1 27 October 2005, Glasgow Sheriff Court, A7444/04.
2 25 July 2005, Peterhead Sheriff Court. A59/99.
3 27 October 2005, Glasgow Sheriff Court, A7444/04.
4 In fact it seems that more than one such notice was served. Why there was more than one is unclear, but it does not seem that anything turned on the point.
5 Ie applications under the Conveyancing and Feudal Reform (Scotland) Act 1970 s 24.

18 February 2002 and that (a) the defender is in default within the meaning of condition 9(1)(a) of the standard conditions as set out in Schedule 3 to the Conveyancing and Feudal Reform (Scotland) Act 1970 and the pursuers are entitled to all of the remedies available to them in terms of Section 20 of and Schedule 3 paragraph 10 of said Act and (b) the pursuers are entitled to enter into possession of the heritable subjects referred to in the Standard Security known as and forming 43 Sherbrooke Avenue, Glasgow and to sell same; (2) ordains the defender to vacate said subjects and to flit and remove himself, his family, dependants, employees, tenants, sub-tenants and others, whomsoever, with their whole gear and belongings furth and from the subjects and to leave the subjects void and redd and that under pain of summary ejection and grants warrant to Officers of Court to summarily eject the defender, his family, dependants, employees, assignees, disponees, agents, licensees, tenants, sub-tenants and whomsoever else may be in or on the subjects; and finds the defender liable to the pursuers in the expenses of the action as taxed; allows an account thereof to be given in and remits same, when lodged, to the Auditor of Court to tax and to report thereon.

The defender pled that on the date of the calling-up notice nothing was due and resting owing, since the pursuer had not made any demand for payment under the guarantee. The calling-up notice, it was argued, did not itself amount to such a demand since it did not mention the guarantee.

The sheriff did not accept this defence and pronounced decree in favour of the pursuer. The *ratio* of the decision is perhaps open to debate, but it seems to have been that a debt does not have to be due and resting owing in order for it to be called up. The sheriff quotes the defender's plea that 'when the said Calling-Up Notice was served, there was no present obligation upon the Defender to make payment to the Pursuers in terms of the Guarantee' and comments:[1]

> In my opinion, the short answer to the proposition advanced within the final section of the foregoing passage of averment is that, in the context of the present action, a 'present obligation to make payment' was not required.

If this passage says what it seems to say, then the state of the law can hardly be satisfactory. Consider a simple example. Jack lends Jill £100,000, interest to be paid quarterly, and the principal to be repaid on the third anniversary of the loan. The loan is secured by standard security. Jill pays the interest punctually each term and quarter day. After 18 months Jack says he wants his money back and when Jill refuses he serves a calling-up notice on the ground that the debt exists, even although it is not due and resting owing. On the sheriff's reasoning, if we have understood him correctly, the calling-up notice is valid and the standard security can be enforced.

With respect we do not think that this can be the law. Section 19 of the Conveyancing and Feudal Reform (Scotland) Act 1970 sets out the way in which a creditor can serve a calling-up notice, but it says nothing about when he becomes entitled to call up. We suggest that the reason for the silence is not far to seek: a creditor becomes entitled to serve a calling-up notice when the

---

1 Paragraph 2.

secured debt has become due and resting owing. The sheriff concludes from an examination of the authorities that 'the calling-up procedure under the 1970 Act does not necessitate that prior constitution of the debt or debts embraced by the sums specified in the calling-up notice or notices served'.[1] This is true. But 'constitution' means constitution by decree of court or by registration for execution in the Books of Council and Session.[2] That, however, was not the point at issue.

Although the above appears to have been the principal *ratio* of the decision, the sheriff also seems to have taken the view that the sums secured by the guarantee were in fact due and resting owing after all, the reason being that the guarantee contained a clause of consent to registration – even though there was no suggestion that the guarantee was ever in fact registered. In the sheriff's view, 'a prior demand for payment is not required where the relevant deed contains a consent-to-registration clause'.[3] This view is based on a passage in Gloag:[4]

A cautionary obligation, originally contingent, becomes a pure obligation by the principal debtor's default, and may then be at once enforced by summary diligence, if the bond by which it is constituted contains a consent to registration for execution. If there is no such clause, it would appear that, even if the cautioner's obligation is to pay on demand, he is entitled to reasonable notice.

Our reading of this passage is that if there is no clause of registration, the cautioner need not pay immediately on demand but must be given a reasonable opportunity to find the money, but that if there is such a clause, he must pay on demand. Whether this is truly the law of Scotland is an interesting question, which we will not go into here. But if it is, then as applied to the facts of the present case it meant merely that the defender was bound to pay immediately on demand. But that point could not help the pursuer, for the defender's case was not that he should be allowed time to pay, but that he had never been asked to pay.

Whether the calling-up notice itself could be construed as a demand under the guarantee is an interesting question, but it seems that no decision was made on this point. The calling-up notice is not quoted in the judgment and so it would be difficult to offer a view.[5]

Whose debts?

In *Bank of Scotland v Forman*[6] the pursuer raised an action to enforce a standard security over the defender's home. The debt in question was owed by a company

---

1 Paragraph 8.
2 Or Sheriff Court Books.
3 Paragraph 10.
4 W M Gloag, *The Law of Contract* (2nd edn 1929) p 708.
5 *Royal Bank of Scotland plc v Lyon*, 20 July 2004, Aberdeen Sheriff Court, digested as *Conveyancing 2004* Case (39), is a case where very little was held sufficient to amount to a demand under a guarantee.
6 25 July 2005, Peterhead Sheriff Court, A59/99.

called Norlea Developments Ltd, which had gone into liquidation. There were three strands of defence. The first was that the debt was not in fact owed by Norlea Developments Ltd but by an associated partnership called Forman & Angus. The second was that the action was based on a calling-up notice that had been served in 1998. Since a calling-up notice lapses after five years,[1] this one had lapsed in 2003. The third defence was that the action was framed on the basis that the defender was personally liable for the company's borrowings. But examination of the standard security itself and relative personal bond showed that, while the standard security secured the borrowings of the company, there was nothing to support the assertion that the defender had any personal liability for those borrowings.

On the first point no decision was made. But the sheriff[2] sustained the second and third lines of defence and dismissed the action. The action was raised in 1999 and so is yet another example of how long-drawn-out litigation often is nowadays.[3] And indeed since the result was dismissal not absolvitor the pursuer would be free to raise a new action framed in different terms.

The case is important because it decides that the raising of an action does not interrupt the running of the five-year period during which a calling-up notice is valid. But the case is also instructive because it illustrates a point about which muddle is very common indeed.

Suppose a bank is to lend money to Sam Swan Ltd, whose sole shareholder and sole director is Sam Swan. The bank wants Sam to grant a standard security over his house to secure the loan. There are no fewer than three ways in which this might be done:

(1) Sam grants a cautionary obligation to the bank in respect of Sam Swan Ltd's borrowing. Sam then grants a standard security in respect of the obligations which he, Sam, has to the bank.

(2) Sam grants to the bank a standard security in respect of the obligations which Sam Swan Ltd has to the bank.

(3) Sam grants a cautionary obligation to the bank in respect of Sam Swan Ltd's borrowing. Sam then grants to the bank a standard security in respect of the obligations which Sam Swan Ltd has to the bank.

In practice these are often treated as if they were interchangeable, but they are not. In the first type, the security granted by Sam secures his *own* obligation, in the sense that it is an obligation for which he himself is personally liable. In the second type, the security secures the debts of Sam Swan Ltd. Sam has signed nothing to make himself personally liable. He cannot be sued for a penny

---

1 Conveyancing and Feudal Reform (Scotland) Act 1970 s 19(11).
2 Sheriff M P Anderson.
3 For other such cases this year see *PIK Facilities Ltd v Shell UK Ltd* [2005] CSOH 94 (running since 1998), *Cahill's Judicial Factor v Cahill* 2 March 2005, Glasgow Sheriff Court, A2680/94 (running since 1994), and the English case of *Hilton v Barker Booth & Eastwood* [2005] 1 WLR 567 (running since 1993). How much has changed since *Bleak House*?

– though if the company does not pay the bank Sam will lose the property. The third type is a mix of the first and second types.

The second type, sometimes called third party security, was the type of security that was used in the *Forman* case. In that case the personal bond signed by the defender ran:

> I ... bind myself ... to pay to the ... Bank of Scotland ... all sums ... that may become due to the bank ... by me ... whether as principal or surety...[1]

This boils down to the vacuous 'I owe what I owe', but vacuous bonds are standard in banking practice. It did not bind the defender to pay anyone else's debts. As for the standard security, in its original form it was for 'all sums due and that may become due ... by me in terms of the personal bond by me in favour of the bank'. This, however, was later varied to add in sums due by Norlea Developments Ltd to the bank, but nothing was added to make the defender liable for Norlea Developments Ltd's borrowings. The sheriff therefore held, correctly in our view,[2] that this was 'third party security, that the defender had no personal liability, and that the bank's action was thus misconceived'. The action was therefore dismissed as irrelevantly pled.

Of course the fact that the granter has no personal liability does not in itself make a security unenforceable, so that the possibility presumably remains open that the bank could still enforce the security provided that it did so in the correct manner. Whether any such attempt will be made remains to be seen. Since the property in question was residential, the Mortgage Rights (Scotland) Act 2001 would apply.[3]

As with so many cases about the enforcement of standard securities, the headline message is for court practitioners but the underlying message is about drafting. Two key questions that drafters must ask themselves are: (1) who is to be personally liable for what debts? and (2) whose debts are to be secured by the security?

LAW OF THE TENEMENT

Necessary repairs

Thomas Dagg & Sons Ltd v Dickensian Property Co Ltd[4] already has an old-fashioned – one is tempted to say Dickensian – feel to it. It concerned repairs which were carried out to a tenement in Glasgow. It seems that the titles were silent as to how decisions on repairs were to be reached,[5] but as the parts in question were common

---

1 It is curious that the Bank of Scotland chooses 'surety', a technical term of English law, for purely Scottish transactions.
2 Cf G L Gretton and K G C Reid, *Conveyancing* (3rd edn 2004) para 19-09.
3 It had not applied in the present action because that action was raised before the Act was passed.
4 2005 GWD 6-84.
5 For otherwise it is difficult to see why the doctrine of necessary repairs had to be invoked. The state of the titles does not, however, appear from the judgment.

property, any owner had power to instruct such repairs as were necessary and to recover from the other owners. That is a general principle of the law of common property.[1] In the event, the owners – as owners usually do – attempted to achieve agreement, but to no avail. The defender, one of the owners, was strongly opposed to the repairs, dismissed the factors, and refused to pay. This action for payment of some £10,000 was the result.

The nub of the dispute was whether the repairs were 'necessary', for, if they were not, there would be no right to recover from the defender. A proof disclosed that there had been severe weathering and erosion through to a vent in a mutual chimney head, that two chimney heads were in a dangerous condition, that cement skews were cracked where the slats met the end of the tenement, and that a dormer window was open to weather ingress. In those circumstances the sheriff,[2] and on appeal the sheriff principal,[3] held that the repairs were indeed necessary.

One of the arguments for the defender had been that it was proper to consider whether, having regard to the age and condition of the building, the repairs had been worth carrying out at all. If the answer was no, they could not be said to be 'necessary'. The sheriff principal rejected this argument:[4]

> No authority was advanced for the view that repairs which are obviously required to preserve the integrity of a building cease to be 'necessary' because it would be economically sensible to demolish. To take that approach would involve considerations of a whole range of factors, not least of which would be the implication of planning controls and relocation of businesses. In a situation where steps are required to prevent water penetration, and to eliminate danger from collapsing chimneys, it seems to me that *prima facie* that is a case of 'necessary' repair in the sense that it would be unrealistic to expect continued use or occupation of the building without the requisite steps being taken to remedy the problems.

A necessary repair, on this approach, need not be a sensible one. But it is a repair which requires to be done if the building is to continue to be used.

The case was decided under the old law. The position under the Tenements (Scotland) Act 2004 would be different. On the one hand, the doctrine of necessary repairs is abandoned.[5] All that matters, under the Tenement Management Scheme, is that a majority of owners is willing to agree to the repairs.[6] But on the other hand, a decision to carry out repairs – a so-called 'scheme decision' – can be challenged by an application to the sheriff within 28 days of the meeting in which the decision was taken, or if the dissenting owner did not attend the meeting (or if there was no meeting) within 28 days

---

1 K G C Reid, *The Law of Property in Scotland* (1996) para 25.
2 Sheriff W Holligan.
3 Sheriff Principal Edward F Bowen QC.
4 Paragraph 19.
5 Tenements (Scotland) Act 2004 s 16.
6 Tenement Management Scheme rr 2.5, 3.1(a). The Tenement Management Scheme ('TMS') is set out in sch 1 of the 2004 Act.

of notification of the decision.[1] In considering such an application the sheriff is directed to do precisely what the sheriff principal declined to do in *Dagg*. Section 5(6) provides that:

> Where such an application is made as respects a decision to carry out mainten-ance, improvements or alterations, the sheriff shall, in considering whether to make an order under subsection (5) above [ie to annul the decision], have regard to –
> (a) the age of the property which is to be maintained, improved or, as the case may be, altered;
> (b) its condition;
> (c) the likely cost of any such maintenance, improvements or alterations; and
> (d) the reasonableness of that cost.

The policy behind the provision is explained in the report by the Scottish Law Commission which gave rise to the legislation:[2]

> If the application for review is in respect of a decision to carry out maintenance, the sheriff should have particular regard to the age and condition of the tenement, to the likely cost of the work, and to whether the cost of the work is reasonable. Thus, if a tenement has deteriorated to the point where it can no longer be economically repaired, the court may readily conclude that to carry out any maintenance at all is to throw good money after bad. Similarly the perfectionism of the majority in insisting on a repair being carried out to the highest possible standard may seem unreasonable, particularly if a cheaper repair would produce a result which was almost as durable.

Reasoning of this kind would no doubt have been of interest to the un-successful defender in *Dagg*. It might even be that the result of that case, under the new law, would have been different.

The non-paying owner

The statutory Tenement Management Scheme ('TMS') applies to all tenements except to the extent that the titles make alternative provision.[3] One effect of the TMS is to remove the veto of individual owners. Instead the rule is majority decision-making: if the owners of a majority of the flats make a 'scheme decision' to carry out a repair, the repair can go ahead, and the fact that an owner objects, or cannot be contacted, does not matter.[4] But the problem remains of recovering the cost. Although the recalcitrant or absent owner is bound to pay his or her

---

1 Tenements (Scotland) Act 2004 s 5.
2 Scottish Law Commission, Report on the *Law of the Tenement* (Scot Law Com No 162, 1998; available on www.scotlawcom.gov.uk) para 5.22.
3 Tenements (Scotland) Act 2004 s 4.
4 Tenement Management Scheme rr 2.5, 3.1(a).

share in the same manner as any other owner,[1] in practice it may be impossible to extract the money – or at least to do so without litigation. What then? Two possible solutions are available, one under the Tenements (Scotland) Act 2004 and a second – a new one – under the Housing (Scotland) Act 2006.

The first solution is for the other owners to grit their teeth and apportion the irrecoverable share amongst themselves.[2] That does not preclude the possibility of eventual recovery against the defaulting owner. But it disposes of the problem in the short term.

The second solution is both new and novel. Section 50 of the Housing (Scotland) Act 2006, when it comes into force, will allow the owners to ask the local authority to pay the missing share.[3] If the local authority agrees, it will pay the share and then seek its recovery from the owner,[4] if necessary by a new statutory security known as a 'repayment charge'.[5] But s 50 applies only if the owners have taken advantage of the provision in the TMS[6] by which the money can be collected before the repair begins.

The procedure is as follows. Under the TMS the owners can make a scheme decision[7] to collect repairs money in advance.[8] This is done by sending to each owner a written notice requiring that the appropriate sum be deposited in a maintenance account. The notice must contain certain information. Section 50(5) of the Housing Act – duplicating, more or less, the relevant provision of the TMS[9] – lists the information as:

(a) the maintenance which is to be carried out,
(b) the timetable for carrying out the maintenance, including proposed commencement and completion dates,
(c) the date of any requirement or agreement to carry out the maintenance; and, in the case of an agreement, the names of those by whom it was agreed,
(d) the estimated cost of the maintenance,
(e) why the estimate is considered reasonable,
(f) the apportioned share of the estimated costs attributable to each of the owners,
(g) how that apportionment is arrived at,
(h) the location and number of the maintenance account, and
(i) the date by which the owners are required to deposit the sum representing their respective apportioned shares in the maintenance account.

---

1 TMS r 4.2.
2 TMS r 5.
3 Section 50 in fact applies to 'premises' (defined in s 194(1)) and not just to tenements and so would be capable of including eg terraced houses in which there were shared obligations of maintenance.
4 Housing (Scotland) Act 2006 s 59(1)(b).
5 H(S)A 2006 ss 172 and 173.
6 Or equivalent provisions in the titles.
7 Unless the titles provide otherwise, this is a decision by majority: see TMS rr 1.4, 2.5.
8 TMS r 3.2(c).
9 TMS rr 3.3, 3.4,

If an owner fails to pay his or her share, any other owner can ask the local authority to 'deposit in the maintenance account a sum representing the share of the estimated costs of any owner who has not complied with a requirement to make such a deposit'.[1] Naturally, the local authority must be satisfied that the share is correct, having regard to the titles and the TMS.[2] Further, it requires to be satisfied that:[3]

   (i)   the owner who has not complied with the requirement is unable to do so,
   (ii) it is unreasonable to require that owner to deposit the sum in question, or
   (iii) that owner cannot, by reasonable inquiry, be identified or found.

For that purpose the local authority may request – but not it seems require – defaulting owners to provide information as to their financial circumstances.[4] An owner who can pay but refuses to do so does not fall within the scheme.

The big question, of course, is whether local authorities will in practice be willing to pay. There is no duty to do so: the operative word is 'may', not 'must'.[5] The answer will depend to some degree on the attitude of the Scottish Executive, for by s 50(8) of the Act the local authority is obliged to have regard to any guidance issued by the Scottish Ministers about the exercise of its functions under the provision.

Not everything in s 50 is clear. Under what circumstances, for example, will a local authority regard it as 'unreasonable' for an owner to have to pay?[6] What happens if the estimates are pessimistic and the local authority pays too much? What happens if the missing share is ultimately recovered by the other owners? In the absence of a statutory power, the local authority would need to rely on the common law of unjustified enrichment for the recovery of over-payments. But perhaps it is churlish to criticise. Section 50 is a welcome development. It is to be hoped that local authorities are willing to make use of it.

Maintenance plans

If a tenement is defective or substandard, the local authority can serve a 'defective building notice'[7] or one of the new 'work notices'.[8] But where it is merely in need of a programme of maintenance, local authorities have not hitherto had powers to require that the maintenance be carried out. Such powers are now conferred by the Housing (Scotland) Act 2006 (not yet in force) and, although they apply to houses of any kind, they seem specially directed at tenements.[9]

---

1 Housing (Scotland) Act 2006 s 50(3).
2 H(S)A 2006 s 50(2)(b).
3 H(S)A 2006 s 50(2)(c).
4 H(S)A 2006 s 50(4).
5 H(S)A 2006 s 50(3).
6 H(S)A 2006 s 50(2)(c)(ii).
7 Building (Scotland) Act 2003 s 28.
8 H(S)A 2006 s 30.
9 H(S)A 2006 ss 44, 45.

The process is started by the service on the owners, and their heritable creditors,[1] of a maintenance order.[2] This can be done only where the local authority considers[3]

(a) that any benefit arising from work carried out in pursuance of a work notice or a repairing standard enforcement order[4] has been reduced or lost because of a lack of maintenance, or

(b) that the house has not been, or is unlikely to be, maintained to a reasonable standard.

There is a right of appeal to the sheriff within 21 days of service.[5] The local authority must register the maintenance order in the Land Register or Register of Sasines.[6]

A maintenance order requires the owners to make a maintenance plan to run for a fixed period not exceeding five years. The plan must specify:[7]

- the maintenance which is to be carried out;
- the steps to be taken for such maintenance;
- a maintenance timetable;
- an estimate of the costs and an apportionment of the liability of each owner.[8]

In addition, a plan may also:[9]

- require the appointment of a manager;
- require the opening of a maintenance account and set out the arrangements for its operation.

The plan must be approved by the owners of a majority of the flats.[10] If, nonetheless, the local authority finds the plan unacceptable (or if no plan is prepared), it can reject it and impose a plan of its own.[11] Once the plan is made, it must be registered by the local authority in the Land Register or Register of Sasines.[12] This is to alert potential purchasers, for responsibility for implementation rests with the owners of the flats for the time being.[13] The full cost must be borne by the owners, and any grant by the local authority is limited

---

1 H(S)A 2006 s 62(1)(e), (2).
2 H(S)A 2006 s 42(1).
3 H(S)A 2006 s 42(2).
4 This is an order made under H(S)A 2006 s 24 requiring a private landlord to carry out repairs.
5 H(S)A 2006 s 64(1)(e), (2)(a).
6 H(S)A 2006 ss 61(1)(d), (3), 194(6).
7 H(S)A 2006 ss 43, 44(2).
8 H(S)A 2006 s 44(2) refers to each 'joint' owner. The meaning is obscure.
9 H(S)A 2006 s 44(3). The relationship of s 44(3)(a) to s 44(2) is unclear.
10 H(S)A 2006 s 46(3).
11 H(S)A 2006 s 46(1).
12 H(S)A 2006 s 61(1)(e), (3).
13 H(S)A 2006 s 48(1).

to the expenses of setting up or closing a maintenance account.[1] If the owners default, the necessary work can be carried out by the local authority and the cost recovered,[2] if necessary by a 'repayment charge'.[3]

It would be surprising if maintenance plans turned out to be common. Already the TMS allows maintenance to be carried out promptly and regularly, without intervention by the local authority. No doubt that is how most local authorities would wish matters to be left. As ever, the extent to which voluntary repairs are supplemented by the new compulsory measures will depend on the resources made available for this purpose.

SINGLE SURVEYS AND PURCHASER'S INFORMATION PACKS

So it has happened: compulsory single surveys and purchaser's information packs. The provisions are in part 3 of the Housing (Scotland) Act 2006, although much of the substance is to be in regulations to be made by the Scottish Ministers. Thus at this stage only the outline of the new system exists. Many of the provisions are based on the Housing Act 2004 (England and Wales). Much of the wording is identical.

The core provisions

What are the core provisions? They are in sections 98 and 99(1). The former provides:

> A person who is responsible for marketing a house which is on the market must possess the prescribed documents in relation to the house.

The latter provides:

> A person who is responsible for marketing a house which is on the market must comply with any request by a potential buyer for a copy of any or all of the prescribed documents in relation to the house.

The duty is not to provide *information*. It is a double duty (a) to *possess*, and (b) to *supply* copies of, *documents*. There may have been some confusion, however, in the drafting process, for sections 98 and 99 are headed 'Duty to have *information* about a house which is on the market' and 'Duty to provide *information* to potential buyer' respectively. It is unclear whether this point will turn out to be significant. But in principle 'documents' and 'information' are different.

---

1 H(S)A 2006 ss 48(3), 49(2), 51.
2 H(S)A 2006 ss 49(1), 59(1)(b).
3 H(S)A 2006 ss 172, 173.

In England the term 'home information pack' is being used. In Scotland the Housing Improvement Task Force, who first suggested the idea, used the term 'purchaser's information pack', though perhaps 'purchasers' information pack' would have been better since the pack is for prospective purchasers. In the event, the Act eschews the English 'home information pack' in favour of the snappier and more informal 'prescribed documents'.

The 'prescribed documents'

What is meant by 'prescribed documents'? That is to be laid down in the regulations. Section 104(2) is the framework provision. The 'prescribed documents' may be about any or all of:

(a) the physical condition of a house (including any characteristics or features of the house),
(b) the value of a house, or
(c) any other matter connected with a house, or the sale of a house, that would be of interest to potential buyers.

The regulations can also contain provisions requiring 'that the date to which information in a prescribed document relates is no earlier than the beginning of such period as the regulations may specify before the date on which the house was put on the market', and requiring 'that a prescribed document be prepared by a person of a description specified in the regulations'.

No doubt one of the documents will be the single survey. As for the others, one may refer to the final report of the Housing Improvement Task Force.[1] This proposed the following:[2]

Sellers of residential properties, including Right To Buy and new build homes, should provide a 'Purchaser's Information Pack' that would include standard documents and information for prospective buyers. Sellers would do this before they put their property on the market. The Pack should contain:

• copies of any planning, listed building and building regulations consents and approvals, or a building standards inspection report if the relevant consents cannot be provided

• any guarantees for work carried out on the property (eg damp proofing or rot eradication) and for new properties, copies of warranties and guarantees

• a copy of the land certificate or, where a certificate is not available,[3] at least a summary of common repair and maintenance burdens attached to flatted properties[4]

• a summary of any property management arrangements

• a Coal Authority Report if applicable.

---

1 *Stewardship and Responsibility: A Policy Framework for Private Housing in Scotland* (2003). See *Conveyancing 2003* pp 96–102.
2 Recommendation 34 at p 44.
3 Presumably because the property is still in the Sasine Register.
4 It is striking that the proposal is limited to flatted properties.

To what extent the regulations will reflect these suggestions remains to be seen. As they stand these suggestions may be problematic in a number of respects. How far back do the 'consents' have to go? Because of the risk of contravening the rules, are sellers' agents going to advise that there should be a building standards inspection report in every case? If the property is in the Sasine Register how is the requirement to provide a 'summary' to be satisfied conveniently? Would a photocopy of the burdens writs be acceptable? If a burden is thought to be invalid, should it be included or excluded? In either case there is a risk of being accused of being misleading, for an omitted burden might turn out to be valid while an included burden might turn out to be invalid. If the property is in the Land Register, presumably a photocopy of the land certificate will be acceptable. But what if the land certificate is old? Will the regulations require that a land certificate must be not more than x months or years old? As for guarantees, how far back? What if a guarantee has been lost? Does that mean that the property can never be sold? An affected owner would then regret that he had not obtained unguaranteed work. And what is meant by 'guarantee'? The common law always implies a warranty: is this included? What if the property is being sold by an executor or by a heritable creditor and no guarantees can be found? What happens, more generally, if information in the prescribed documents is inaccurate, or accurate but incomplete?

The Register of Prescribed Documents

The Act authorises the setting up of a new register, the Register of Prescribed Documents'.[1] There will be recording dues to be paid by sellers.

Timing

The prescribed documents must all be ready before the property can go on the market.

If the regulations require that the 'documents' include information about or copies of the land certificate or Sasine deeds, and if those are held by a lender, it will be necessary to request them timeously. Here the slowness of some lenders may cause problems. It may be that non-solicitor estate agents will have greater difficulty than solicitor estate agents in lining up the documents quickly.

Who is responsible?

On whom does the duty fall? Section 106 provides:

---

1 Housing (Scotland) Act 2006 s 104(4).

(1) Only the seller or a person acting as agent for the seller may be responsible for marketing the house.

(2) A seller is not so responsible if any person is acting as agent for the seller.[1]

So in most cases the responsibility falls on the estate agent. If the seller is using a non-solicitor estate agent, the responsibility does not fall on the solicitor.

Is the duty unconditional?

The duty to *have* the documents is unconditional. The duty to *supply copies* of them to prospective buyers is subject to three qualifications. The first is that:[2]

the duty ... does not apply if the person responsible for marketing the house reasonably believes that the person making the request –
(a) is unlikely to have sufficient means to buy the house in question,
(b) is not genuinely interested in buying the house, or
(c) is not a person to whom the seller is likely to be prepared to sell the house.

The second is that 'the person responsible for marketing the house may charge a sum not exceeding the reasonable cost of making and, if requested, sending, a paper copy of any prescribed documents requested'.[3] Payment before delivery can be demanded.[4] One imagines that this right will seldom be invoked. Sellers are usually only too happy to give out gratis copies of sales particulars. If someone looks like a timewaster, the seller has the right to refuse in any case: see above. If a charge is made it includes the cost of photocopying and (where applicable) posting. Whether it would include an overhead for the secretarial time involved in the work is unclear.

The third qualification is that the seller can impose a condition as to 'the use or disclosure of the copy (or any information contained in or derived from it)'.[5]

Property on the 'market'

The rules apply when a property is 'marketed'. They are not tied to a sale. Thus if a property is marketed but never sold, the rules still apply. Equally, if a property is sold without being marketed, the rules do not apply. What does 'marketed' mean? Section 119 says that '[a] house is on the market when the

---

1 See also ss 101, 107 and 108 (noting in particular s 108(4)). There is perhaps an element of repetition in these provisions.
2 H(S)A 2006 s 99(3). Section 99(4) adds that: 'Nothing in subsection (3) authorises the doing of anything which is an unlawful act of discrimination'.
3 H(S)A 2006 s 99(6).
4 H(S)A 2006 s 100(1), (2).
5 H(S)A 2006 s 100(3).

fact that it is or may become available for sale is, with a view to marketing the house, made public in Scotland by or on behalf of the seller.' It adds, helpfully, that '[a] house is to be regarded as remaining on the market until it is sold or taken off the market.'

Right-to-buy sales

The rules do not apply to right-to-buy sales by social landlords, for in such cases the property is not 'marketed'. Nevertheless, s 113 has a special set of rules which apply to right-to-buy sales, applying analogous provisions to them.

What sorts of property?

The rules apply only to 'houses'. 'House'[1]

(a) means any living accommodation which is, or which is capable of being, occupied as a separate dwelling (other than a mobile home or any other living accommodation which is not a building), and

(b) includes –

  (i) any part of the living accommodation (including its structure and exterior) which is, and any common facilities relating to it which are, owned in common with others, and

  (ii) any yard, garden, garage, out-house or other area or structure which is, or which is capable of being, occupied or enjoyed together with the living accommodation (solely or in common with others).

So the sale of purely commercial property is not covered by the legislation. What about the sale of a farm which includes a farmhouse? Presumably it was not intended that such sales be affected, for the legislation was aimed at the residential property market. But if there is a sale of a farm with a farmhouse, the fact that fields are being sold does not alter the fact that a *house* is being sold.

The rules 'apply in relation to a house only when it is available for sale with vacant possession'.[2] Thus if tenanted property is sold, the rules do not apply. A seller who, though an owner-occupier, does not wish to comply with the new system, could presumably get round the new rules by selling subject to a right to stay in the property for a short period after settlement. But one would imagine that this idea would be unattractive to most buyers and so is unlikely to be used.

Duties and sanctions

In England it seems that the duty to provide what is there called the 'home information pack' is owed to prospective buyers: a prospective buyer whose

---

1 H(S)A 2006 s 194(1).
2 H(S)A 2006 s 115(1).

request for the documents is refused, or who receives the documents but considers them disconform to the regulations, has a direct action against the seller.[1] The Scottish provisions impose a duty on the seller (or seller's agent) but do not say to whom the duty is owed. No rights of enforcement are conferred on prospective buyers.

Is this therefore a matter of criminal law? At first sight it might seem that the answer is yes, for breach of the rules may result in a 'penalty charge notice'.[2] But that is merely the wrapping. The 'penalty' is not imposed by any court, but by the authorised officer of the local weights and measures authority.[3]

So the question, to whom is the duty owed?, is not one easily answered. The legislation seems to confer rights on prospective buyers, but in fact such buyers cannot enforce those 'rights'. Nor is this a matter of criminal law. Is the duty owed to the weights and measures authority or its 'authorised officer'?

The person charged (we cannot say 'fined' because this is non-criminal) can appeal to the weights and measures authority. If that appeal fails there is a further appeal to the sheriff court. The 'penalty charge', despite its name, is an ordinary civil debt, so the weights and measures authority can enforce it by an action for payment.[4] The summary warrant procedure is not available for the enforcement of penalty charges.

Comments

From the Official Report of the Scottish Parliament for 24 November 2005:[5]

> **Mary Scanlon:** In addressing the 22 amendments in my name in the group, I am conscious of a comment that the minister made earlier. He said that legislation needs a good evidence base. I thoroughly agree with that, of course. However, the single seller survey pilot started in July 2004, with a target of carrying out 2,000 surveys; the figure of 2,000 was then reduced to 1,200 and, in the end, only 74 single seller surveys were carried out on which to base this legislation.

As these figures indicate, the survey pilot was a failure.[6] Why? 'The feedback gained by the SPCs and individual solicitors in all of the pilot areas is that after having the single survey explained to them, virtually all sellers refused

---

1 Housing Act 2004 s 170.
2 H(S)A 2006 s 111. Earlier it was observed that the Act imposes not a duty to provide *information* but a duty to provide *documents*. The same thinking can be detected here. The sanction for breach is not a 'penalty charge' but a 'penalty charge *notice*'. But presumably it must be implied that if there is a notice *of* a penalty charge there must *be* a penalty charge – even if the Act does not say so.
3 Section 69 of the Weights and Measures Act 1985, as amended, says that 'in Scotland, the local weights and measures authority for the area of each council constituted under section 2 of the Local Government etc (Scotland) Act 1994 shall be the council for that area'.
4 H(S)A 2006 sch 3 para 7(1).
5 Columns 21079–80.
6 For the official evaluation of the pilot, see www.scotland.gov.uk/Publications/2005/09/05165527/55281.

to participate.'[1] One may add that Ministers did not wait to see how the new English rules and 'home information packs', enacted more than a year earlier, would fare. There are puzzles here which we are unable to explain.

Some critics have foretold that the new rules will spell disaster for the housing market. This seems unlikely. People want to buy and sell houses, and it would take a lot more than this to stop them. But 'less than disastrously bad' is less than praise. The opposite possibility is that compulsion will prove a wild success, but this seems just as unlikely.

There are many questions which only time will answer. What, exactly, will the regulations say?[2] How much are single surveys going to cost? Will buyers and lenders be prepared to trust these surveys? Will buyers wish to have their own surveys carried out? Will the new rules raise upset prices, which is something that many politicians seem to want? Will the new rules make fixed-price sales commoner? Will it be harder for financially distressed owners to sell, since they will have to find a substantial sum in advance to pay for the survey? If so, will this trigger an increase in forced sales by mortgage lenders? What will happen when a seller's survey turns out to be defective and a buyer has relied on it? Will the other documents (eg about title conditions or about maintenance history) cause problems, whether practical ones or problems of interpretation? If there are allegedly errors in these other documents will there be civil liability? If so, whose, and on what ground of law? How will the proposed Register of Prescribed Documents work in practice? How much will it cost? What is it for? How seriously are weights and measures departments going to set about their business? Above all, after 10 years will the whole scheme look foolish? To these questions we can offer no answers.

STATUTORY PERSONAL BAR

Stratton (Trade Sales) Ltd v MCS (Scotland) Ltd[3] is a case about leases, but also raises issues of general importance to conveyancers. The core of the dispute was whether a lease existed. The pursuer said it did. The defender said it did not. No deed between the parties had been signed. The alleged lease was for a period of more than one year, so that a signed document was necessary under the Requirements of Writing (Scotland) Act 1995.[4] The pursuer sought to circumvent this difficulty by founding on the statutory personal bar provisions in s 1(3) and (4) of the 1995 Act, whereby the absence of a signed document does not matter if there have been sufficient actings. The provisions are:

---

1 Stewart Brymer, 'Thin edge of the wedge?' (2005) 50 *Journal of the Law Society of Scotland* April/50. For a defence of the compulsory single survey see Lorne Crerar, 'The single survey: why it should be supported' (2005) 50 *Journal of the Law Society of Scotland* Sept/46. For more criticisms see Ian Ferguson, 'Don't make it compulsory' (2005) 50 *Journal of the Law Society of Scotland* June/55 and Stuart Bain, 'Still thumbs down' (2005) 50 *Journal of the Law Society of Scotland* Nov/52.
2 For the draft English regulations, see www.odpm.gov.uk/index.asp?docid=1161272.
3 24 March 2005, Glasgow Sheriff Court.
4 Requirements of Writing (Scotland) Act 1995 s 1(2)(b), (7).

(3) Where a contract ... is not constituted in a written document complying with section 2 ... but one of the parties to the contract ... ('the first person') has acted or refrained from acting in reliance on the contract ... with the knowledge and acquiescence of the other party to the contract ... ('the second person') –
  (a) the second person shall not be entitled to withdraw from the contract ... ; and
  (b) the contract ... shall not be regarded as invalid, on the ground that it is not so constituted, if the condition set out in subsection (4) below is satisfied.
(4) The condition referred to in subsection (3) above is that the position of the first person –
  (a) as a result of acting or refraining from acting as mentioned in that subsection has been affected to a material extent; and
  (b) as a result of such a withdrawal as is mentioned in that subsection would be adversely affected to a material extent.

This says that if (i) there is an unsigned agreement, and (ii) there have then been the relevant actings, the unsigned agreement is binding. Does this mean that you must *first* prove agreement (consensus) and *then* prove the actings? Or might it be sufficient to prove the actings, and then argue that the actings themselves have a double role: they both prove the existence of an agreement and also trigger statutory personal bar? Under the pre-1995 common law rules there had been two cases in which the courts had favoured the latter approach: *Errol v Walker*[1] and *Morrison-Low v Paterson*,[2] the first of which concerned missives and the second a lease.

The present case was under the new, post-1995, law, but in fact the sheriff did not have to make a definite decision. For the pursuer's written pleadings were framed in such a way that they stood or fell on the draft lease, and the difficulty here was that the covering letter for the draft lease said: 'Not Legally Binding: Subject to Conclusion of Formal Missives.' In those circumstances the sheriff held that the draft lease in itself could not amount to an agreement, and, that being so, the pursuer's case failed.

But had the written pleadings been somewhat different, the issue of how the 1995 Act should be interpreted would have been a central one, and the sheriff took the opportunity to offer his views on the broader question:

I therefore tend to the view that, for these specific statutory provisions to apply, there must be (a) an identifiable contract of some sort, followed by (b) relevant and unequivocal actings.... Accordingly, whilst I specifically reserve judgment on this point of statutory interpretation, I am nevertheless reasonably clear that it should not be open to the party proponing the existence of a contract to pray in aid a series of occurrences and, thereafter, to point, inferentially, to a preceding agreement.

---

1 1966 SC 93. It is perhaps surprising that this case was not cited by (or perhaps to) the court.
2 1985 SLT 255. The facts of this case were very special, and perhaps it should not be classified as a personal bar case.

The issue is a difficult one, both in terms of what the law ought to be and in terms of the true textual meaning of s 1 of the 1995 Act. Under the general law, a contract can be constituted by acts as well as by spoken or written words. This happens every day when entirely wordless contracts of sale are entered into at supermarket checkouts. If the view expressed by the sheriff is correct then a distinction falls to be drawn between (a) agreements made in words, whether written or spoken, and (b) agreements made by actings. Such a distinction seems problematic. Yet we would incline to agree that s 1 of the 1995 Act must be read as the sheriff reads it.[1] Section 1(3) says that the actings are to be 'in reliance on the contract' and that would seem to imply that there is *already* an agreement (albeit not binding because unsigned). The defender argued that to allow the actings themselves to be the agreement for the purposes of s 1 would be 'a logical absurdity', and there is very considerable force in that argument. Actings could not be carried out in reliance on an agreement which was itself the *result* of those selfsame actings.

In theory, perhaps, there could be (a) an agreement constituted by the actings of the parties followed by (b) later and separate further actings in reliance on that agreement. But even if that is correct, it would not be an easy case to plead in court.

When an owner gives possession to a potential tenant, and the potential tenant accepts possession, with the terms of the lease still being negotiated, the law will usually imply a one-year lease. But it is not possible to pursue this issue because the opinion issued by the sheriff does not make it clear whether the defender had taken possession, and, indeed, it may be that the pursuer and defender were at odds on this issue.[2]

JUDICIAL RECTIFICATION

Conveyance by way of gift: section 8(1)(b)

The threshold provision for judicial rectification is s 8(1) of the Law Reform (Miscellaneous Provisions) (Scotland) Act 1985. This states that:

> Subject to section 9 of this Act, where the court is satisfied, on an application made to it, that –
>
> (a) a document intended to express or to give effect to an agreement fails to express accurately the common intention of the parties to the agreement at the date when it was made; or
>
> (b) a document intended to create, transfer, vary or renounce a right, not being a document falling within paragraph (a) above, fails to express accurately the intention of the grantor of the document at the date when it was executed,

---

1 We expressed the same view, subject to the adverb 'probably', in *Conveyancing* (3rd edn 2004) para 3–15.

2 The sheriff's judgment proceeded upon a debate on the pleadings, and there had been no proof.

it may order the document to be rectified in any manner that it may specify in order to give effect to that intention.

So far as conveyancing deeds are concerned, an application must usually be taken under para (a) of s 8(1) because such deeds generally implement a prior agreement. But in the case of gifts there is typically no prior agreement and so the relevant provision is para (b). The difference matters. In an application under para (a) it is necessary to show a common intention of the parties, and that that common intention has been departed from in the deed. In an application under para (b) the concern is solely with the intention of the granter. To some extent that makes life easier because it reduces the chance of conflicting evidence. But it may also make life harder because, in the absence of a prior contract, there may be little or nothing in the way of evidence as to the granter's intention.

McEwan's Exrs v Arnot[1] was a case involving para (b). Mrs McEwan decided to give a house to her daughter. Mrs McEwan also owned, and lived in, the house next door. That house derived its services and means of access from the house which was to be the subject of the gift. Yet no servitudes were reserved in the disposition. Mrs McEwan sought the rectification of the disposition to the effect of inserting the necessary servitudes.[2] This involved adding some 650 words to what was not, at present, a long deed. In allowing a proof before answer, the sheriff principal[3] considered the nature of the evidence which was likely to be available.[4] In the first place there would be the instructions which Mrs McEwan had given to her solicitor. Other relevant evidence would be the fact of donation, the fact that at the time of the disposition Mrs McEwan was using all the services in question, and the fact that, without the servitudes, Mrs McEwan's house might be unmarketable.

Error in expectation

McEwan's Exrs v Arnot[5] raised another point of importance. It was clear from Mrs McEwan's averments that she had neither instructed her solicitors to reserve the servitudes, nor given them sufficient other information from which the need for such servitudes might have been deduced. So there was no error in expression as such: on the contrary, the disposition was in exactly the form instructed by Mrs McEwan. That, argued the daughter, was fatal to the case for rectification, for it could never be a relevant basis for a claim under s 8(1)(b) that the granter had failed properly to communicate her intention to the drafter of the document. This argument was rejected by the sheriff principal. In a key earlier decision, *Bank of Ireland v Bass Brewers Ltd*,[6] it was held, in effect, that rectification is capable of

1 11 February 2005, Perth Sheriff Court, A516/01.
2 Separately, she sought to argue that the servitudes could in any event be implied. See p 89.
3 Sheriff Principal R A Dunlop QC.
4 Paragraph 20.
5 11 February 2005, Perth Sheriff Court, A516/01.
6 2000 GWD 20-786, 2000 GWD 28-1077, discussed in *Conveyancing 2000* pp 118–119.

encompassing errors in expectation. So if the parties intend legal effect X and the document actually brings about legal effect Y, there is a failure of a type which can be rectified under s 8.[1] That was the case here. Mrs McEwan – or so it was averred – intended that the disposition should reserve servitudes. Because she had not given the relevant information to her solicitors, the disposition did not do so. Hence it was capable in principle of being rectified. A proof before answer was allowed.

McEwan's Exrs is the first case to apply the decision in *Bank of Ireland*. As the facts demonstrate, it suggests that s 8 is capable of being used to make far-reaching changes to a deed.

Protection of third parties

Even where s 8 plainly applies, it does not follow that rectification will be granted. That depends on whether, and if so how, third parties will be affected.

Jones v Wood[2] illustrates the issues and also develops the law. The facts speak to a conveyancing disaster. The owners of a farm divided it into two parts. One part, comprising the farmhouse, steading and some land, was sold to the pursuers. The rest of the land was sold to someone else. Unfortunately the plans in the dispositions were defective in that almost an acre was omitted from the pursuers' plan and included instead on the plan attached to the disposition of the farmland. Although the missing acre included buildings, the mistake was not noticed at the time. The pursuers' disposition was granted, and registered, first. In due course a land certificate was issued. Naturally enough, the acre was also missing from the title plan. The purchasers of the farmland sold on within a few months to a third party who likewise registered his disposition. The land certificate issued in his favour included the missing acre.

When the mistake was discovered the pursuers sought to put matters right, but the third party – now registered as owner of a windfall acre – was unwilling to relinquish his gain. In those circumstances the pursuers raised an action in which they sought (i) rectification of the plan attached to their disposition so as to restore the missing acre and, consequentially, (ii) rectification of their title sheet to the same effect.[3]

It is worth pausing to consider the consequences in property law of these craves. Rectification – both of the deed[4] and, in this isolated case only,[5] of the Land Register – is retrospective, so that, if granted, the effect is as if the deed and Register had always been in those terms. In many respects this rewriting

---

1 G L Gretton and K G C Reid, *Conveyancing* (3rd edn 2004) para 17-07.
2 [2005] CSIH 31, 2005 SLT 655.
3 Note that only the first of those is judicial rectification under s 8 of the Law Reform (Miscellaneous Provisions) (Scotland) Act 1985. The second is rectification of the Land Register by the Keeper, under s 9 of the Land Registration (Scotland) Act 1979.
4 Law Reform (Miscellaneous Provisions) (Scotland) Act 1985, s 8(4); but see also s 9(4).
5 Rectification of the Land Register is not usually retrospective, but there is a special rule where this follows on from judicial rectification of a deed: see Land Registration (Scotland) Act 1979, s 9(3A).

of history is puzzling and illogical. In the present case it operated to the pursuers' benefit.[1] For if the missing acre could be added, retrospectively, to the disposition, the result would be to make the later disposition of the farmland, also retrospectively, *a non domino* in respect of the acre. Both title sheets would then be inaccurate, the pursuers' for including too little and the third party's for including too much. The missing acre could be added to the pursuers' title sheet, and removed at the same time from the third party's. Rectification of the Register would be possible in the second case because it was the pursuers, and not the third party, who were in possession and so there could be no question of prejudice to a proprietor in possession.[2]

In principle, the case for rectification of the deed was overwhelming. The missives included the acre. The disposition did not. There was no suggestion that the parties had changed their minds between missives and disposition, and indeed the pursuers had taken, and kept, possession of the acre. The omission in the disposition, in short, was no more than a conveyancing blunder – exactly the sort of mistake which s 8 is designed to correct. Initial opposition to the application on its merits was not persevered with.

There was, however, a complication. The missing acre had not simply been retained by the granter of the deed, as might have happened. Instead it had been conveyed, along with the farmland, to someone else, and that person had in turn conveyed it to a third party. Third parties, reasonably enough, are protected against rectification, by s 9 of the 1985 Act. In order to qualify for that protection it is necessary to show both good faith (ie absence of knowledge, actual or constructive, that the deed was inaccurate), and also knowledge of and reliance on that deed in its unrectified state. Importantly, good faith by itself is not enough.

Jones turned on questions of knowledge and reliance. The relevant provision is s 9(2) of the 1985 Act:

> Subject to subsection (3) below, this section applies to a person (other than a party to the agreement or the grantor of the document) who has acted or refrained from acting in reliance on the terms of the document or on the title sheet of an interest in land registered in the Land Register of Scotland being an interest to which the document relates, with the result that his position has been affected to a material extent.

After a proof, the sheriff had held that there was no reliance.[3] Accordingly, rectification was allowed. The Extra Division has now confirmed that view. It is true that the third party's solicitor had examined the pursuers' disposition so that the third party, through his solicitor, could be regarded as familiar with its contents.[4] That, however, was not enough. What was needed, according to

---

1 If rectification were not retrospective, it would have been necessary for the pursuers to seek rectification also of the two dispositions of the farmland, because, for as long as they stood, the pursuers' disposition as rectified only prospectively would have been *a non domino* in respect of the missing acre.

2 Land Registration (Scotland) Act 1979, s 9 (1), (3).

3 27 October 2003, Dumfries Sheriff Court. For a discussion, see *Conveyancing 2003* pp 104–106.

4 Presumably the disposition was examined only because, in view of the quick resale following first registration, no land certificates were yet available.

the Extra Division, was not merely a general acquaintance with the deed but specific reliance on the defectively expressed term itself (ie the description in which the acre was omitted). No such specific reliance could be shown. The land was being acquired for forestry. The third party had no interest in the missing acre or in the buildings on it, and no reason for noticing their omission from his neighbours' deed. Nor had he changed his position as a result for, on the evidence, he would have bought the land at the same price even if the boundaries in the pursuers' disposition had been correctly drawn. Given that the value of a property is normally reduced if part of it is removed from the title, that conclusion is perhaps surprising, but reliance is a matter of fact and there had been a proof. In approaching s 9(2) in this way, the Extra Division was following the decision of Lord Nimmo Smith in an earlier case, *Sheltered Housing Management Ltd v Cairns*.[1]

Interaction with the Land Register

As more and more titles are taken on to the Land Register, it becomes increasingly likely that rectification of dispositions will affect not only one registered title but two. It is not clear that the legislation, which was produced mainly with contracts in mind, is able to cope with this complexity. The difficulties are illustrated by a variant on the facts of *Jones v Wood*.[2]

Suppose Alan is the registered owner of land. He dispones some of the land to Brenda. A new title sheet is made up for Brenda's land, and the land is removed from Alan's title plan. In the event it turns out that too little land was conveyed to Brenda, and that both title plans are, in that sense, wrong and vulnerable to judicial rectification. Meanwhile Alan dispones the rest of his land to Colin, who is registered as owner in Alan's place. Brenda, discovering the error, seeks judicial rectification of the disposition in her favour to the effect of adding in the missing land. In addition she seeks rectification (in the Land Register sense) both of her own title sheet (to add the missing land) and of Colin's title sheet (to remove the land). Brenda has never possessed the missing land. It was possessed first by Alan and is now possessed by Colin.

At first sight, it seems that Colin has nothing to fear. He bought his land on the basis of Alan's land certificate. The missing land was duly shown on the title plan. Colin is the registered owner of that land, and in possession of it. He is in good faith. On normal principles of registration of title, his position is invulnerable, for there can be no rectification of the Register against a proprietor in possession who is neither fraudulent nor careless.[3] Indeed any other result would undermine the whole basis of conveyancing with registered land.

But the position is more complex, and less certain, than at first appears. In seeking rectification of the Register against Colin, Brenda will rely on s 9(3)(b) of the Land Registration (Scotland) Act 1979. This provides, so far as relevant, that:

---

1 2003 SLT 578, discussed in *Conveyancing 2002* pp 97–100.
2 [2005] CSIH 31, 2005 SLT 655, discussed above.
3 Land Registration (Scotland) Act 1979 s 9(3)(a).

if rectification under subsection (1) above would prejudice a proprietor in possession –

...

(b) the court or the Lands Tribunal for Scotland may order the Keeper to rectify only where ... the rectification is consequential on the making of an order under section 8 of the Law Reform (Miscellaneous Provisions) (Scotland) Act 1985.

In other words, if the court rectifies Brenda's disposition, it can also make any 'consequential' alterations on the Register as may be necessary; and in that event there is no protection for a proprietor in possession. Worse still, no indemnity is payable, since s 12(3)(p) expressly removes any entitlement in the situation just described. Thus Colin would lose the disputed land (which he possesses) without compensation. Of course, it is possible to argue that rectification of *Colin's* title sheet is not 'consequential' on the judicial rectification of the disposition in favour of *Brenda*. But probably that argument would not succeed, because it is rectification of Brenda's disposition which makes Colin's disposition *a non domino* in respect of the disputed land and hence makes his title sheet inaccurate. And even if it did succeed, Brenda could seek the judicial rectification of Colin's disposition as well, on the basis of s 8(3) of the 1985 Act which allows for the rectification of 'any other document ... which is defectively expressed by reason of the defect in the original document'.

If, therefore, Colin cannot resist rectification of his title sheet, he must seek to prevent the judicial rectification in the first place. That in turn means that he must rely on the third party protection given by s 9 of the 1985 Act. The crucial provision is s 9(2), which was quoted earlier. In order to succeed, Colin must show that he acted *in reliance on* the document which is to be rectified (ie Brenda's disposition) or on 'the title sheet of an interest in land registered in the Land Register of Scotland being an interest in land to which the document relates'. Plainly, Colin did not rely – did not see even – Brenda's disposition at the time he bought his land from Alan. His examination of title will have been confined to Alan's land certificate. But a land certificate is not a 'title sheet' but merely a copy of one; and even if this difficulty can be surmounted, it is not clear whether *Alan's* title sheet is, as s 9(2) requires, a title sheet of an interest in land to which *Brenda's* disposition 'relates'. If not, Colin has no defence to the rectification of Brenda's disposition.

We would argue that s 9(2) of the 1985 Act should be interpreted so as to allow reliance on Alan's land certificate. But even in that case there can be no certainty that Colin's defence would succeed. As already mentioned, an acquirer of land is normally safe if in good faith and in possession. To this s 9(2) adds a requirement of reliance. And, following the decision in *Jones v Wood*, Colin must be able to show that he knew (through his solicitors) that the land certificate included the disputed land and that he would not have proceeded with the acquisition (or at least not at that price) had the land not been included.

It would be wrong to exaggerate the difficulties just described. It will be a rare purchaser of land who is faced with a title challenge which derives from the rectification of a deed in favour of a different person; and even where such a challenge arises the prospects of a successful defence under s 9 of the 1985 Act may be reasonably good. Nonetheless, the provisions of s 9 do not fit easily with protection of *bona fide* proprietors in possession which is the key idea of registration of title; and as a result in at least some cases a *bona fide* proprietor in possession will lose land without payment of indemnity.

GRATUTIOUS ALIENATIONS AND THE NEED FOR REGISTRATION

When does ownership of land pass? This issue has been troubling the Scottish legal system for many years. We have had *Sharp v Thomson*[1] and we have had *Burnett's Tr v Grainger*,[2] and we have had rivers of academic ink. In *Accountant in Bankruptcy v Orr*[3] the issue came up again albeit in different guise. Although a bankruptcy case, it has much of interest for conveyancers.

Alistair Orr owned a house at 117 Dudley Avenue, Leith, where he lived with his wife, Margaret Orr. On 6 August 1992 they signed this:

> WHEREAS the First Party holds the title to the subjects known as 117 Dudley Avenue, Edinburgh (the subjects) CONSIDERING that the Second Party has resided with the First Party for a considerable number of years FURTHER CONSIDERING that the First and Second Parties agree that the Second Party is entitled to a One half share of the subjects FURTHER CONSIDERING that the reversionary interest[4] in the subjects is approximately £50,000 and the First and Second Parties have agreed that should the subjects be sold each party would receive the sum of TWENTY FIVE THOUSAND POUNDS (£25,000) STERLING, FURTHER CONSIDERING that the First Party wishes to raise funds on his share of the reversionary interest in the subjects to the extent of TWENTY FIVE THOUSAND POUNDS (£25,000) STERLING THEREFORE IT IS AGREED as follows:
>
> (1) The First Party shall grant a Disposition in favour of the Second Party of a one half share of the property.
> (2) The Parties shall grant a Standard Security in favour of the Bradford and Bingley Building Society for the sum of FIFTY THOUSAND POUNDS (£50,000) STERLING.
> (3) The First Party shall grant a Disposition in favour of the Second Party of his reversionary interest in the subjects.

Pursuant to this agreement, two dispositions were signed. One was a disposition by Mr Orr to Mrs Orr of a one-half share. The second was a disposition by him to her of the other half share. These dispositions were both signed on the same day as each other and the same day as the agreement, ie 6 August 1992. Why there were two dispositions rather than one is unclear.

---

1 1997 SC (HL) 66.
2 2004 SC (HL) 19.
3 [2005] CSOH 117, 2005 SLT 1019.
4 What 'reversionary interest'? None has been mentioned. The narrative states that 'the First Party holds the title'.

There are other oddities in the agreement. For example, while it is provided that a standard security for £50,000 would be granted to Bradford and Bingley Building Society, it is not said whether this was to secure an existing loan, or a new loan which the parties hoped to raise. Nor is anything said as to the mutual liability of the parties for the loan. It is not clear how this security relates to the 'funds' that the first party is said to wish to raise 'on his share of the reversionary interest in the subjects'.[1]

It is stated that 'the Second Party is entitled to a one half share of the subjects' but it is not explained why. Nor is it explained why, if Mrs Orr was entitled to a one-half share, she was not to receive a half share but the whole. Nor is it clear why, if Mrs Orr is to become sole owner, 'the First and Second Parties have agreed that should the subjects be sold each party would receive the sum of … £25,000.' Nor is it clear what would happen to the excess if the property were to be sold for more than that sum.

In the narrative there is a 'reversionary interest', followed by a 'share of the reversionary interest' and in clause 3 an obligation to dispone a 'reversionary interest' which seems to equate not with the 'reversionary interest' but with the 'share of the reversionary interest'. And while at clause 3 there is an obligation to dispone a 'reversionary interest', at clause 1 there is an obligation to dispone 'a one half share of the property' which presumably is something other than a 'reversionary interest'. (Actually the term 'reversionary interest' is one that needs to be handled with care. If an owner of property grants a standard security, the right he has thereafter is still the real right of ownership. The creditor's right is a subordinate real right. The term 'reversionary interest' obscures the real situation and is usually best avoided. Indeed, the word 'interest' itself needs to be used with caution.) This is a deed that we are not able to understand.

The two dispositions were recorded on 13 January 1995, ie about two and a half years later. It is not clear why there was such a delay. It is unclear whether the standard security in favour of the Building Society, signed on the same day as the two dispositions, was recorded. But we do know that Mrs Orr was considering seeking 'indemnity against the third parties who acted as her agents, on the basis that they failed timeously to register the dispositions'.[2]

Mr Orr was sequestrated on 12 March 1998. His trustee raised an action to reduce the dispositions as being gratuitous alienations. The cut-down period for gratuitous alienations is either two years or five years,[3] the longer period being applicable where the grantee is an 'associate' of the debtor.[4] Clearly Mrs Orr fell within the definition of an 'associate'. The five-year period thus stretched back to 1993. If the dispositions were effective as from 6 August 1992 (the date of execution and, presumably, delivery), they would be immune. But if they

---

1 One possibility is that this was to be his half of a loan from the Bradford and Bingley Building Society. But this seems unlikely since there is no parallel statement about Mrs Orr.
2 Paragraph 4.
3 Bankruptcy (Scotland) Act 1985 s 34.
4 Defined in the Bankruptcy (Scotland) Act 1985 s 74.

were effective as from 13 January 1995 (the date of recording), they would be presumptively reducible.

One line of defence was that the dispositions were not in fact gratuitous. The 1992 agreement had stated that Mrs Orr was 'entitled' to a half share. It was averred that before the property was bought, the parties had been co-owners of another, and that the proceeds of the sale of that property had been used to buy the new one. Such situations do sometimes arise, and when they do it is desirable that there be documentation to record the intentions of the parties. Is one party making a gift to the other or merely a loan? In the Inner House decision of *MacFadyen's Tr v MacFadyen*[1] a mother and her son bought a house together. Later the son disponed his share to the mother without payment. Later still he was sequestrated, and his trustee sought reduction of the transfer. The mother pled that the transfer was not gratuitous since the price had been wholly paid by her. This defence was dismissed and reduction was granted. In the light of this decision, it was held that Mrs Orr could not be regarded as having given any 'consideration' for the transfer. This sort of situation – where a disposition appears to be gratuitous, or at least at undervalue, but is later alleged to have been in consideration of some debt – is quite common. Another example from the present year is *Henderson v 3052775 Nova Scotia Ltd*.[2]

We would pause for a moment to consider this issue further. In *MacFadyen's Tr* the mother presumably had a claim against her son for half the price. The claim would be an unjustified enrichment claim. But this point was, it seems, not put to the court in *MacFadyen's Tr*. Nor, apparently, was any argument based on unjustified enrichment put forward in the present case. Now, an enrichment claim would have been a claim to a sum of money, not a claim to half the property.[3] But even so, there might be an argument that the transfer was not gratuitous, on the basis that the half share was being conveyed for a price, namely the surrender of the enrichment claim. To make this clearer, take the following example. Jack and Jill acquire title to a house. Jill pays the whole price (£200,000). Later, when the property is worth £250,000, Jack dispones his share to Jill. It could be argued that he owed her £100,000, under the law of unjustified enrichment,[4] and, further, that in exchange for the disposition, she is giving up her claim against him, the net result being that the disposition was not gratuitous. It would be an interesting argument, but rather a long shot. One difficulty is that Jack is conveying an asset worth £125,000, so arguably there is still a gratuitous alienation. Another is that in practice such documentation as exists is unlikely to set forth matters in a manner consistent with the argument.

In fact there is something to be said for structuring the deal in the way just suggested. For example, Jack could sign a promissory note to Jill for £100,000. The disposition would narrate a price of £100,000. There would be a simultaneous minute of agreement agreeing that Jack's debt to Jill (the promissory note)

---

1 1994 SC 416.
2 [2005] CSIH 20, digested above as Case (47).
3 See *Conveyancing 2004* p 65–66.
4 We cannot here enter into the strengths and weaknesses of this argument. If Jack and Jill are married the issues become even more complex because of the mutual obligations of aliment.

would be set off against Jill's debt to Jack (price for the half share). Of course there would also be drawbacks in this way of proceeding, including SDLT and registration expenses. In practice such considerations may make the parties opt for a gratuitous structure, but the dangers of such a structure must be borne in mind and, indeed, ought to be explained to Jill.

One other practical point in cases of this sort is that timeous registration is, as ever, important. In a sale, if the disposition is registered before the disponer is sequestrated the disponee is safe. But in a gratuitous transfer the registration of the disposition starts a wait-and-see period of either two or five years.

We return to the case. The defender had another line of argument. This was that ownership had passed when the disposition was delivered in 1992: 'on delivery, the transferor could be said to lose rights of ownership ... following delivery of a disposition, the disponer could be said to have no beneficial interest in the property.'[1] In the light of *Burnett's Tr v Grainger*[2] it was perhaps inevitable that this plea would fail. As a matter of fact, the legislation on gratuitous alienations has a specific provision for how a transaction should be dated. Section 34(3) of the Bankruptcy (Scotland) Act 1985 provides that 'the day on which an alienation took place shall be the day on which the alienation became completely effectual'.[3] The words 'completely effectual' are broad because they have to cover a variety of situations, not only the transfer of land, but in relation to land the natural, and accepted, interpretation would be the date of registration.[4] Not surprisingly, the Lord Ordinary pronounced decree of reduction as concluded for.

STAMP DUTY LAND TAX[5]

Introduction

Quite apart from any legislative changes, the basic administration of SDLT continued to cause enormous practical and administrative problems throughout 2005. Once one moves beyond basic purchases and some new leases, there can be great difficulty not only in working out what the tax should be, but also in completing the forms and especially in getting the certificate back. Nothing which has been done in new legislation in 2005 will make this any easier.

Admittedly, the introduction of e-filing (which happened just before the end of the year) is already assisting administration considerably: put simply, the quite unacceptable delay in the issue of certificates in even the most basic of transactions will become much less common. But Her Majesty's Revenue and Customs have too much faith in electronic systems, a faith which is all the more surprising given its unhappy experience with a range of computer efforts. Thus

---

1 Paragraph 9.
2 2004 SC (HL) 19.
3 The same is true for companies: Insolvency Act 1986 s 242(3).
4 *Grant's Tr v Grant* 1986 SC 51, decided under predecessor legislation..
5 This part is contributed by Alan Barr of the University of Edinburgh.

it was no surprise to anyone that the SDLT electronic reporting system 'went down' just before Christmas; and that among the bizarre advice on offer was to submit returns from home, in the middle of the night, as it would be easier to get through. Things may improve on the administrative side, but new legislation means that the complications of the tax have become worse, not better.

In the medium to long term, the introduction of e-conveyancing will solve at least some of the administrative problems affecting SDLT. There are some pathfinder provisions for the new system in the year's legislation.[1]

Election years tend to bring not one but two Finance Acts and 2005 was no exception. The excuse used to be that there were measures which absolutely had to be put through and others which could await careful consideration by a new Parliament. But this excuse has almost disappeared with what appears to be the complete lack of parliamentary scrutiny of any kind (and certainly a lack of considered, non-Government amendments) which afflicts revenue legislation these days. The first Finance Act 2005, rushed through in a matter of hours, was actually a little longer than Finance (No 2) Act 2005; and both contained changes to SDLT.

Threshold for residential property

It is perhaps unsurprising that, in an election year, the increase in the domestic threshold was among the first batch of changes enacted (and was virtually the only one actually announced by the Chancellor). The basic change is simple: a doubling of the threshold for residential properties from £60,000 to £120,000.[2] This change affects both purchases and leases, which must take virtually all Scottish residential leases outwith the possibility of a charge. It applies to transactions with an effective date on or after 17 March 2005.[3]

It is worth a reminder that mixed properties are not residential, so there may be some merit on occasions in separating out titles of suitable properties.

Abolition of disadvantaged areas relief for non-residential property

Much less prominence was given to the abolition of disadvantaged area relief for commercial property.[4] This is, in effect, an extremely serious rise in tax for such properties in large areas of the country, most of which will involve payment of SDLT at the highest rate (4%). The sums raised certainly exceed any overall savings from the rise in the residential threshold.

This change was brought into effect on Budget day, but the relief was pre-served for the settlement or substantial performance of contracts entered into on or before 16 March 2005, provided that there was no variation or assignment of the contract or sub-sale of the property and that the transaction was not the exercise of an option or right of pre-emption.[5] These transitional provisions, like

---

1 Finance (No 2) Act 2005 s 47.
2 Finance Act 2003 s 55(2), sch 5 para 2(3), amended by the Finance Act 2005 s 95(1), (2).
3 Finance Act 2005 s 95(4).
4 Finance Act 2005 s 96, sch 9.
5 Finance Act 2005 sch 9 para 4.

those on the introduction of SDLT itself, will cause careful examination of a range of old contracts to see if what is being done can fall within their terms.

Alternative property finance

The rules on so-called Islamic mortgages are recast.[1] The effect of this reorganisation is, partly, to divide the relevant provisions into two separate regimes. Finance Act 2003 s 72 now applies only in relation to land in Scotland and provides for schemes involving the sale of land to financial institutions and leased to individuals. Section 72A is new and again applies only in relation to land in Scotland. This envisages a different scheme, whereby the financial institution and the individual enter into common ownership of the land. The first of these schemes is also covered for England and Wales and Northern Ireland in separate legislation. Section 73, which applies to all three United Kingdom jurisdictions, covers the case where land is initially sold to a financial institution and later resold to the individual, with a standard security granted back.[2]

The schemes have in common the provision of an exemption for one step in a series which avoids the need to charge interest, or at least the appearance of interest. They are not, in terms, restricted to persons whose beliefs do not allow interest to be charged and thus are at least in theory available to anyone who is able to enter into the appropriate arrangement with a financial institution. They are, however, restricted to individuals – which indicates that, for this purpose at least, a company or other non-natural person must be assumed not to have the possibility of a conscience or a religious belief.

As part of a range of anti-avoidance measures, Finance Act 2003 s 45(3) is amended so that sub-sale relief is not available where the relief under s 73 for alternative finance mortgages is also claimed in the same transaction.[3]

Anti-avoidance: disclosure

The Government is close to being obsessed with tax avoidance. Vast tracts of legislation are devoted to attempts to stamp it out, and it could reasonably be said that the whole edifice of SDLT was created as part of the anti-avoidance agenda.

Part of that agenda involves disclosure of tax avoidance schemes to Her Majesty's Revenue and Customs. As a result of that disclosure, loopholes are closed by yet more complex legislation and the whole vicious circle spins again. This disclosure regime started with value added tax and income tax in relation to employee matters and 'financial products'. In Finance Act 2004, legislation

---

1 Finance Act 2003 ss 71A–73, amended by the Finance Act 2005 s 94, sch 8. For a discussion of some versions of Islamic mortgages in Scotland see Graham Burnside, 'Unveiling the Islamic mortgage' (2005) 50 *Journal of the Law Society of Scotland* Dec/58.
2 The Conveyancing and Feudal Reform (Scotland) Act 1970 s 9(3) prohibits the vesting of title to heritable property in a lender as a security for a loan. Of the three types of scheme (s 72, s 72A and s 73) the third seems not to come into conflict with s 9(3), but with the first two a question might possibly arise.
3 Finance (No 2) Act 2005 s 49, sch 10 para 2.

was introduced to pave the way for a disclosure regime to be extended to all taxes.[1]

The 2005 Budget included an announcement[2] that the regime was to be extended to SDLT:

> The new rules will ensure promoters or users provide details to the Inland Revenue of schemes and arrangements whose use might be expected to provide, as a main benefit of using the scheme, an SDLT advantage concerning property which:
> - is not residential property (as defined in section 116 FA 2003); and
> - which has a market value of at least £5 million.
>
> The Inland Revenue will not issue a reference number for such schemes and a promoter will have no obligation to convey a reference number to a client. Consequently, in most cases users of a scheme will have no obligation to provide the Inland Revenue with information. But in some circumstances the users themselves will be required to provide information about the scheme. This is where:
> - the promoter is offshore;
> - the user has devised the scheme in-house; or
> - the promoter is a lawyer who cannot make a full disclosure without revealing legally privileged material.
>
> In the last case the client can choose to waive the right to privilege and allow the lawyer to make the disclosure.

This was followed by regulations which set out prescribed arrangements for the purposes of SDLT.[3] These regulations came into force on 1 August 2005 and set out the scheme as explained in the Budget announcement. However, they also set out a range of arrangements which are excluded from being prescribed (and thus reportable) unless such arrangements are used in conjunction with each other.

Thus the mere claim to a relief, on its own, is not notifiable; nor even is the acquisition of land by a special purpose vehicle or the sale of its shares. But when these steps are combined, then the 'scheme' does become notifiable.[4]

Generally under the disclosure rules, lawyers cannot be compelled to provide the Revenue with information. The Revenue believes that the client must then do so, but that is at least open to some doubt.

Certainly, these new rules will require at least some attention in any large commercial case where SDLT saving is attempted, although the position will probably settle down in due course.

Anti-avoidance: other provisions

As well as the important general development just described, there were a number of specific anti-avoidance changes in the second 2005 Finance Act. Brief details follow.

---

1 Finance Act 2004 ss 306–319.
2 Inland Revenue, *Rev BN97* paras 5–6.
3 Stamp Duty Land Tax Avoidance Schemes (Prescribed Descriptions of Arrangements) Regulations 2005, SI 2005/1868.
4 Ibid, sch.

Changes to the group relief provisions in Finance Act 2003 sch 7 part 1[1]

Under the rules before this change, group relief was clawed back if the transferee company ceased to be a member of the same group as the transferor company within three years of the transfer. This was subject to various let-outs, for example where the transferor left the group in certain circumstances. The new rules extend the circumstances in which clawback will occur. Notably, the circumstances in which clawback will occur because of a change of control of the transferee company are extended.

There is a further, much more general, change to the rules on group relief. In keeping with other tax provisions for group relief, a general rule excluding it is inserted, where the transaction is not effected for *bona fide* commercial reasons, or where it forms part of arrangements of which the main purpose, or one of the main purposes, is the avoidance of liability to (virtually any) tax.[2] This new provision is well known elsewhere in tax legislation, but its familiarity does not make it any easier to prove (for example) that things were not done with a tax-saving motive in mind. It seems to be another attempt to prevent avoidance, as well as evasion, throughout the tax system.

This is at least capable of catching innocent transactions; in any company sale, an SDLT history in relation to previous transfers and group relief claims may be necessary.

Changes to the acquisition relief provisions in Finance Act 2003 sch 7 part 3

Similar changes as apply to group relief are made to the rules on the withdrawal of acquisition or reconstruction relief where rent is involved as consideration and in relation to the need for a commercial purpose for such arrangements.[3]

More fundamental changes are made to this relief as it affects what might be described as 'property undertakings'. The legislation[4] currently refers to an 'undertaking'. The new provisions require that the 'undertaking' must be a trade and must not be a trade consisting wholly or mainly of land transactions.[5] It was always a little doubtful the extent to which the undertakings relief applied to undertakings which consisted, essentially, of let investment properties. This makes it clear, now, that it does not.

Partnership transactions

Changes are made to the already extremely complex charges on partnership transactions. There is a new charge where land is transferred into a partnership and the transferor takes money out of the partnership within three years[6] – a

---

1 Finance (No 2) Act 2005 sch 10 paras 3–7, 19.
2 See Finance Act 2003 sch 7 para 2(4A) (as inserted).
3 Finance (No 2) Act 2005 sch 10 para 20.
4 Finance Act 2003 sch 7 para 8.
5 Finance (No 2) Act 2005 sch 10 para 8.
6 Finance Act 2003 sch 15 para 17A, inserted by the Finance (No 2) Act 2005 sch 10 para 10.

change which will certainly catch innocent transactions. The idea is that the transferor has put land in – at which time there may or may not have been a tax charge – and there is then, within three years of the introduction of the land, a withdrawal of funds from the partnership by that transferor, the funds being other than a mere payment of income profits to the transferor. The withdrawal of funds becomes a deemed land transaction (and it is worth emphasising that at this time there is nothing that could be thought of as a movement of property in *any* sense – certainly not a conveyance and probably not any form of partnership accounts adjustment). The 'purchasers' will be the partnership, and the consideration the amount of the withdrawal. There is, however, a credit for the SDLT paid (if any) when the land was transferred to the partnership, and an absolute restriction on the amount chargeable to the market value at the time of the transfer into the partnership.

Transactions by or with bare trustees so far as they affect the grant of new leases

The provisions of para 3 of sch 16 to the Finance Act 2003 (which provide that the acts and property of a bare trustee are attributed to the beneficiary) are not to apply to the grant of a lease.[1] In other words, the fact that one of the parties to a lease is a bare trustee will be ignored in determining the charge on its grant. This will prevent the use of leases to bare trustees in certain tax planning schemes involving leases. It is a reminder of the difficulties surrounding the use of bare trustees in general – not to mention the grave doubts which exist in Scotland about transactions between bare trustees and beneficiaries.

Lease variations

The rules on lease variations are changed yet again, so that where the tenant pays for any variation in the lease after 19 May 2005, that payment is at least potentially liable to SDLT.[2]

Contingent consideration in the form of a 'loan' or 'deposit'

A change is made to the rules on leases by the insertion of a new para 18A into Finance Act 2003 sch 15A.[3] This is aimed at what might be thought of as purely avoidance transactions, where sale consideration is disguised as an apparent loan. After some representations, this change was restricted so as to exclude at least some loan or deposits of a 'normal' amount, which might be used to secure dilapidations or other payments due to the landlord.[4]

---

1 Finance (No 2) Act 2005 sch 10 paras 11, 12.
2 Finance Act 2003 Sch 17A para 15A(1A), inserted by the Finance (No 2) Act 2005 sch 10 para 13.
3 By Finance (No 2) Act 2005 sch 10 para 14.
4 See Finance Act 2003 sch 17A para 18A(3) (as inserted).

Definition of 'company' in relation to transactions involving public bodies

A change is made to Finance Act 2003 s 66 which has the effect of restricting the relief given by that provision[1] to companies established by local authorities to genuine, 'Companies Act' companies, as opposed to the wider definition of corporate bodies used for 'company' elsewhere in the legislation.[2]

---

1 The relief is for land transactions entered into, or in consequence of, or in connection with, a reorganisation effected by or under a statutory provision if both purchaser and vendor are public bodies.
2 Finance Act 2003 s 66(6), inserted by the Finance (No 2) Act 2005 sch 10 para 18.

⊰ PART V ⊱

TABLES

TABLES

CUMULATIVE TABLE OF APPEALS 2005

This lists all cases digested in *Conveyancing 1999* and subsequent annual volumes in respect of which an appeal was subsequently heard, and gives the result of the appeal.

Adams v Thorntons
2003 GWD 27-771, OH, 2003 Case (46) *affd* 2004 SCLR 1016, 2005 SLT 594, IH, 2004 Case (44)

Anderson v Express Investment Co Ltd
2002 GWD 28-977, OH, 2002 Case (5) *affd* 11 Dec 2003, IH, 2003 Case (13)

Armstrong v G Dunlop & Sons' JF
2004 SLT 155, OH, 2002 Case (48) *affd* 2004 SLT 295, IH, 2003 Case (39)

Burnett v Menzies Dougal
2004 SCLR 133 (Notes), OH, 2004 Case (42) *rev* [2005] CSIH 67, 2005 SLT 929, 2005 Case (40)

Burnett's Tr v Grainger
2000 SLT (Sh Ct) 116, 2000 Case (21) *rev* 2002 SLT 699, IH, 2002 Case (19) *affd* 2004 SC (HL) 19, 2004 SLT 513, 2004 SCLR 433, HL, 2004 Case (24)

Caledonian Heritable Ltd v Canyon Investments Ltd
2001 GWD 1-62, OH, 2000 Case (69) *rev* 2002 GWD 5-149, IH, 2002 Case (61)

Caterleisure Ltd v Glasgow Prestwick International Airport Ltd
2005 SCLR 306, OH, 2004 Case (21) *rev* [2005] CSIH 53, 2005 SLT 1083, 2005 SCLR 943, 2005 Case (15)

Cheltenham & Gloucester plc v Sun Alliance and London Insurance plc
2001 SLT 347, OH, 2000 Case (63) *rev* 2001 SLT 1151, IH, 2001 Case (73)

Conway v Glasgow City Council
1999 SCLR 248, 1999 Hous LR 20 (Sh Ct) *rev* 1999 SLT (Sh Ct) 102, 1999 SCLR 1058, 1999 Hous LR 67, 1999 Case (44) *rev* 2001 SLT 1472, 2001 SCLR 546, IH, 2001 Case (51).

Glasgow City Council v Caststop Ltd
2002 SLT 47, OH, 2001 Case (6) *affd* 2003 SLT 526, 2004 SCLR 283, IH, 2003 Case (6)

Grampian Joint Police Board v Pearson
2000 SLT 90, OH, 2000 Case (18) *affd* 2001 SC 772, 2001 SLT 734, IH, 2001 Case (17)

Hamilton v Mundell; Hamilton v J & J Currie Ltd
20 November 2002, Dumfries Sheriff Court, 2002 Case (13) *rev* 7 October 2004, IH, 2004 Case (11)

Henderson v 3052775 Nova Scotia Ltd
2003 GWD 40-1080, OH, 2003 Case (58) *affd* [2005] CSIH 20, 2005 Case (47)

Inverness Seafield Co Ltd v Mackintosh
1999 GWD 31-1497, OH, 1999 Case (19) *rev* 2001 SC 406, 2001 SLT 118, IH, 2000 Case (13)

Jones v Wood
27 October 2003, Dumfries Sheriff Court, 2003 Case (52) *affd* [2005] CSIH 31, 2005 SLT 655, 2005 Case (42)

Kaur v Singh (No 2)
1999 HousLR 76, 2000 SCLR 187, 2000 SLT 1324, OH, 1999 Case (34) *affd* 2000 SLT 1323, 2000 SCLR 944, IH, 2000 Case (26)

Kingston Communications (Hull) plc v Stargas Nominees Ltd
2003 GWD 33-946, OH, 2003 Case (35) *affd* 2005 SC 139, 2005 SLT 413, IH, 2004 Case (31)

Labinski Ltd v BP Oil Development Co
2002 GWD 1-46, OH, 2001 Case (16) *affd* 2003 GWD 4-93, IH, 2003 Case (17)

McAllister v Queens Cross Housing Association Ltd
2001 HousLR 143, 2002 SLT (Lands Tr) 13, 2002 Case (26) *affd* 2003 SC 514, 2003 SLT 971, IH, 2003 Case (28)

Minevco Ltd v Barratt Southern Ltd
1999 GWD 5-266, OH, 1999 Case (41) *affd* 2000 SLT 790, IH, 2000 Case (36)

Moncrieff v Jamieson
2004 SCLR 135, Sh Ct, 2003 Case (20) *affd* [2005] CSIH 14, 2005 SC 281, 2005 SLT 225, 2005 SCLR 463, 2005 Case (6)

Robertson v Fife Council
2000 SLT 1226, OH, 2000 Case (84) *affd* 2001 SLT 708, IH, 2001 Case (82) *rev* 2002 SLT 951, HL, 2002 Case (69)

Royal Bank of Scotland plc v Wilson
2001 SLT (Sh Ct) 2, 2000 Case (53) *affd* 2003 SLT 910, 2003 SCLR 716, 2004 SC 153, IH, 2003 Case (40)

Scottish Youth Theatre (Property) Ltd v RSAMD Endowment Trust Trustees
2002 SCLR 945, OH, 2002 Case (3) *affd* 2003 GWD 27-758, IH, 2003 Case (8)

Souter v Kennedy
23 July 1999, Perth Sheriff Court, 1999 Case (69) *rev* 20 March 2001, IH, 2001 Case (81)

Spence v W & R Murray (Alford) Ltd
2001 GWD 7-265, Sh Ct, 2001 Case (9) *affd* 2002 SLT 918, IH, 2002 Case (1)

Stevenson v Roy
2002 SLT 445, OH, 2002 Case (67) *affd* 2003 SC 544, 2003 SCLR 616, IH, 2002 Case (54)

Tesco Stores Ltd v Keeper of the Registers of Scotland
2001 SLT (Lands Tr) 23, 2001 Case (30) *affd* sv *Safeway Stores plc v Tesco Stores Ltd* 2004 SC 29, 2004 SLT 701, IH, 2003 Case (25)

Thomas v Allan
2002 GWD 12-368, Sh Ct, 2002 Case (7) *affd* 2004 SC 393, IH, 2003 Case (22)

Wilson v Inverclyde Council
2001 GWD 3-129, OH, 2001 Case (29) *affd* 2003 SC 366, IH, 2003 Case (27)

TABLE OF CASES DIGESTED IN EARLIER VOLUMES BUT REPORTED IN 2005

A number of cases which were digested in *Conveyancing 2004* or earlier volumes but were at that time unreported have been reported in 2005. A number of other cases have been reported in an additional series of reports. For the convenience of those using earlier volumes all the cases in question are listed below, together with a complete list of citations.

Adams v Thorntons WS
2005 SC 30, 2005 SLT 594, 2004 SCLR 1016

Canmore Housing Association Ltd v Bairnsfather
2004 SLT 673, 2005 SCLR 185

Caterleisure Ltd v Prestwick International Airport Ltd
2005 SCLR 306

Hallam Land Management Ltd v Perratt
2005 SCLR 230

Kingston Communications (Hull) plc v Stargas Nominees Ltd
2005 SC 139, 2005 SLT 413

Perth and Kinross Council v Scott
2005 SLT 89, 2005 SCLR 297

Whitbread Group plc v Goldapple Ltd
2005 SLT 281, 2005 SCLR 263